The ABC's of VBS

how it can work for you!

by ELEANOR DANIEL

illustrated by Mary Ann Dorr

STANDARD PUBLISHING
Cincinnati, Ohio   3201

Library of Congress Cataloging in Publication Data

Daniel, Eleanor Ann.
  The ABC's of VBS.

  Bibliography: p.
  1. Vacation schools, Christian.   I. Title.
II. Title: A B C's of V.B.S.
BV1585.D34   1984   268   83-5049
ISBN 0-87239-705-X

© 1984 by The STANDARD PUBLISHING Company, Cincinnati, Ohio
Division of STANDEX INTERNATIONAL Corporation
Printed in U.S.A.

PREFACE

A long time ago I attended my first VBS. As a junior-high youngster, I enjoyed it, but was totally unaware of the planning and preparation that had gone into making it the enjoyable experience it was. Sometime later I directed my first VBS and got a taste of the time and effort that go into a successful VBS program. A few years later I taught my first college-level class—Vacation Bible School—and emphasized to the students the need to plan and prepare well.

It is now fifteen college classes and sixteen Vacation Bible Schools later. The forms have changed somewhat, publicity reflects new ideas, the audience is wider in age range, and a greater variety of ideas have been introduced than when I first knew about VBS and began to teach in it. But this book still emphasizes the same theme as did that first college class: VBS is almost always a success when it is carefully planned, prayerfully prepared, and positively promoted. VBS is still VBS, whatever the changes—a special Bible teaching time well worth the tireless efforts and countless hours spent in preparing to teach so that those who come may be introduced to the Lord Jesus Christ.

CONTENTS

Chapter 1

VBS—PAST, PRESENT, AND FUTURE

As you read, think about the following:
1. What are the values of a VBS program?
2. Who was the founder of the VBS movement?
3. What are the major developments in the history of the VBS movement?
4. What two principles did Homer Grice contribute to VBS?
5. Who introduced the first VBS program?
6. What future can be predicted for the VBS movement?

Take some warm summer days. Add a good measure of energetic boys and girls. Stir in committed teachers who have prepared well. Add a large portion of the Bible, a bit of crafts, several songs, a dab of lively activities. Mix these together for five to ten days, and the result is Vacation Bible School, an adventure in Bible learning.

VBS has been described in a variety of ways. But describe it as you will, it has an irreplaceable function in reaching and teaching God's Word to boys and girls. Change as it has and will, it continues to occupy an invaluable place in the church's overall ministry.

Vacation Bible School is a school of Christian education for all ages conducted by the church. It is a *Vacation* Bible School because it is usually held during the summer school vacation. It is Vacation *Bible* School because the curriculum is (or should be) centered in the Word of God. It is Vacation Bible *School* because it contains some elements of a school: teachers and pupils, a definite curriculum, and systematic instruction.

Vacation Bible School is a ministry. Churches that have designed and developed a program to reach the community have achieved their goals. For example, two small congregations in western Illinois recognized the ministry potential of VBS and set out to make their ministries to their communities. Both succeeded, each penetrating its small community to touch families, then nurturing those contacts into response to the Word of God and growing maturity in Christian living. Each experienced threefold numerical growth in the Sunday services, not to speak of the personal spiritual growth in many individuals.

VBS should be an integral part of the total ministry of the church—not an afterthought, an appendage, nor an unsupervised hodgepodge of activity. For a VBS to be genuinely successful, it must be a carefully designed part of a total teaching program of the local church. That means that it is authorized by the church, directed by the church, staffed by the church, financed by the church, and used by the church to reach, teach, win, and develop people for Jesus Christ.

VBS—Its Values

The accrued values of a good VBS are well worth the energy, effort, and money put into it. The list should include at least the following:

1. VBS provides a time of concentrated Bible study. Most church programs for Bible study meet but weekly, leaving a seven-day span for material to be forgotten. But the typical VBS meets daily for a week or two at a time, providing as much instruction in a week as would usually occur in thirteen weeks in Sunday school, thus building day-by-day upon previous learning.
2. VBS provides a unique opportunity to teach the unchurched—both adults and children. It is somehow easier to get unchurched families to enroll their children first in VBS than it is in Sunday school. For some reason, it

seems to be less threatening. At the same time, the emphasis on activity makes VBS appealing to unchurched youngsters. Churches need to create opportunities for contact for this very reason.

3. VBS helps adults find, use, and develop their special gifts. More than one person has taught his first Bible lesson at VBS. Many first played the piano for a group, led singing, or taught crafts in VBS. It is a good place to assimilate new people into the ministry of the church, allow them to develop confidence, and send them on to yet more responsible ministries.

4. VBS is set in an atmosphere where new ideas can be tried. Because VBS is a short-term project, it is a prime place to introduce new organizational ideas, teaching techniques, or scheduling procedures. Once they work there, it is often easier to incorporate those innovations into other programs.

5. VBS builds enthusiasm. Children usually enjoy it. Teachers who have had a positive experience talk about it. Unchurched people come. Enthusiasm is the result.

A Grand Heritage—a Promising Future

Those who have grown up going to VBS often take it for granted, thinking little about its origin. VBS, however, has a rich history that needs to be appreciated.

Probably the earliest Vacation Bible School was conducted in First Church of Boston in 1866. There is no record, however, of the subsequent fate of that program. Another such VBS was conducted in Montreal in 1877. Again, there is no record of later programs to follow it up.

Then in 1894, Mrs. D. G. Miles, the wife of a minister in the small central Illinois community of Hopedale, conducted a VBS in a public park. She enrolled thirty-seven pupils whom she charged a one-dollar enrollment fee. A success, it is considered by some to be the documented beginning for the VBS movement. Again, however, the subsequent history of that school is not recorded. Yet these first schools were vital forerunners of the VBS movement.

In 1898, Eliza Hawes, superintendent of the children's department at the Epiphany Baptist Church in New York City, became increasingly concerned about the neglected children of the East Side slum area. (Her motivation was not unlike that of Robert Raikes when he founded the first Sunday school in England.)

Mrs. Hawes developed what she called Everyday Bible School, a program that lasted for six weeks. The only facility she could find was a beer parlor, which she rented for twenty-five dollars per month. The program lasted for two hours each day and included worship, music, Bible stories, drawing, Bible memorization, nature study, marching games and exercises, salutes to the flag, and handwork, even cooking and sewing for the girls. For seven years she conducted her program for unchurched children with the support of her minister, until she moved to Charlottesville, Virginia, to live.

In 1901, Dr. Robert Boville, corresponding secretary for the New York Baptist Mission Society, learned of Mrs. Hawes' program. He recommended the program to many churches and officially inaugurated the VBS movement. The response to the VBS idea was overwhelmingly successful, largely because it gave idle children something constructive to do during the summer.

Boville, in 1907, set up the National Vacation Bible School Committee, that later became the Daily Vacation Bible School Association. It was reorganized in 1916 as the International Association of Daily Vacation Bible Schools. Then in 1922, Dr. Boville founded the World Association of Daily Vacation Bible Schools to give emphasis to promoting schools in the Far East.

Another forerunner that should be mentioned is the summer parochial school conducted by Lutheran and Reformed churches for immigrants prior to World War I. These were language and Bible schools aimed primarily at Swedish immigrants. The schools waned after World War I, however, largely because of anti-German sentiment by Americans. (Swedish is a Germanic language.)

It was only a matter of time until denominations and church groups adopted VBS as a means of Christian education. The Presbyterian Church of the U.S.A. made VBS a part of its denominational emphasis on Christian education in 1910. The Northern Baptist Convention did the same in 1915. Standard Publishing Company, an independent publisher established in 1866, began producing VBS materials in 1922.

VBS work among the Southern Baptist Convention was adopted in 1924, when Homer Grice of Washington, Georgia, was called to develop their VBS ministry. He retained this position until 1953. He wrote *The Vacation Bible School Guide,* a work that served as the basic methods book for Southern Baptists from 1924 to 1956. Grice laid down two basic principles for VBS work that have given direction to other church groups besides Southern Baptists.

1. A VBS was to be church-centered, i.e., it was to be promoted, operated, and financed by a local church who would use the program to achieve its goals.

2. Volunteer workers were essential. Grice knew very well that the genius of the Sunday-school movement resided in its volunteer workers who were deeply committed to Bible teaching. He insisted that VBS should be no different.

Once VBS became an accepted part of the Christian education scene, curriculum materials became a pressing need. Standard Publishing introduced the very first VBS program in 1923. It was a five-week course for kindergarten through Juniors. They added materials for Intermediates in 1929. These materials were reprinted until 1948 when a new graded ten-day course was introduced, followed by introduction of a single-theme curriculum in 1952.

Scripture Press, founded in 1933 in Chicago, produced its first VBS course in 1940. Concordia marketed a three-week program in 1947, and Gospel Light, also founded in 1933, entered the VBS market in 1951. Denominational headquarters also produced VBS materials. By the mid to late 1960's, these publishers, along with Standard, were marketing both five- and ten-day materials.

By 1982, Standard alone was reaching over three million VBS pupils in its publishing efforts. Add to that number the work of the other independent publishers and the denominational efforts and you begin to catch a vision of the magnitude of the VBS ministry.

And what of its future? Will VBS continue to be the same effective tool that it has been to the present?

VBS has been a flexible tool. Though there are many similarities between Mrs. Hawes' first VBS and one conducted today, the changes are also evident. VBS is shorter in length now, but probably with little significant loss of ministry because of more extensive youth and camping programs than there were in the past. Now VBS often meets at night, allowing inclusion of a far wider age group than in 1898. Today's VBS sometimes moves out of the church building into backyard settings in an effort to penetrate neighborhoods evangelistically. For a time, evangelistic emphasis seemed to wane in many churches, but a recent resurgence of interest has changed that. All in all, VBS has been a wonderfully flexible tool. The future is bright as churches catch a vision of the magnitude of the VBS ministry.

Summary

Throughout its rich history, Vacation Bible School has been successful when it has existed to minister to people. It is a unique opportunity to reach the unsaved and to involve the learner in a time of concentrated Bible study. From a program designed to reach slum children, VBS has developed into a meaningful part of the church's total Christian education ministry. The future must be claimed by those who would continue to use the summer to reach, teach, win, and develop for Christ.

Project

Draw a historical profile of VBS in your congregation: date of its beginning, objectives, special features, attendance patterns, and how it has changed through the years.

Bibliography

Burcham, Arthur and Cox, William R. *Working in Vacation Bible School.* Nashville: Convention Press, 1975.

Burnett, Sibley C. *Better Vacation Bible Schools.* Nashville: Convention Press, 1957.

Butt, Elsie Miller. *The Vacation Church School in Christian Education.* New York: Abingdon Press, 1957.

Getz, Gene. *The Vacation Bible School in the Local Church.* Chicago: Moody Press, 1962.

Jantz, Stan N. "A Brief History of VBS." *The Bookstore Journal.* January, 1976.

Person, Peter P. *An Introduction to Christian Education.* Grand Rapids: Baker Book House, 1963.

Stout, John E. and Thompson, James V. *The Daily Vacation Church School.* New York: Abingdon Press, 19 .

Weidman, Mavis Anderson. "Vacation Bible Schools." *An Introduction to Evangelical Christian Education.* Edited by J. Edward Hakes. Chicago: Moody Press, 1964.

Westing, Harold J. "VBS—How It's Changing With the Times." *The Bookstore Journal.* February, 1982.

Chapter 2

DEVELOP A PLAN OF ACTION

As you read, think about the following:
1. What are some goals suitable for VBS?
2. When is the best time to have VBS? What determines the answer?
3. How long should VBS be? What determines the answer?
4. Outline proper space, size, and teacher/pupil guidelines.
5. List five principles for effective VBS organization.
6. What is a planning calendar? Why is it important?

VBS is a ministry—an influential, life-changing ministry. It has the potential for penetrating a community, touching lives for Christ, and shaping the future. Those results are well within the grasp of all leaders who carefully plan and meticulously implement the program.

The leader of a successful VBS program needs to consult with the elders of the church and/or the Christian Education Committee to lay initial plans for the program. Some preliminary decisions must be made before staff is recruited, curriculum selected, schedules outlined, or publicity designed. Some of those decisions need approval of supervising groups; others merely need to be planned out personally to give direction to future decisions and planning. Those preliminary decisions are outlined in this chapter.

Set Goals

The first step to a successful VBS is to set goals, to determine what this program should accomplish. Clearly defined goals are a must, if energy and resources are to be used with greatest efficiency. This must be done with intention, not merely by default.

Some churches unfortunately have no greater purpose than merely conducting VBS because they have "always had one." The goal is to get through it, nothing more or less. Not

13

so surprisingly, that is about the extent of what the VBS accomplishes. Yet it need not be that way. VBS can achieve some worthwhile goals.

Evangelism and outreach must remain a major goal of VBS. VBS allows unique opportunities to reach those who are unreachable by a traditional Sunday program. Children who face a long summer with little structured activity welcome a chance to do something interesting. Parents do not have to alter schedules a great deal to get their youngsters to VBS; some welcome direction for their children's energy. These are prime contacts. If those who attend are followed up with an evangelistic ministry to the family, outreach will be achieved and souls may be won to Christ.

Bible teaching is a second major goal. Bible truths need to be introduced and reinforced. Both the saved and the unsaved should be confronted by Bible truth, a goal that will become a reality only when careful planning is done.

Family ministry is a worthwhile goal selected by many congregations. It is implemented in a variety of ways, but the intent is to make VBS a ministry to the entire family. Though this may be an overarching concern, it still should not alter the dual goals of evangelism and teaching.

Other goals may become paramount. Some churches intend to do the bulk of missions' education through their VBS. Others make a heavy emphasis on recreation or crafts or music. All of these are legitimate concerns if they are subordinate to the broader goals of evangelism and teaching.

This step of setting goals is critical. If the goal is family emphasis, organizational patterns and publicity must reflect that. If outreach is a major goal, then choice of curriculum and publicity emphases are clearly affected as well as, perhaps, the time of day chosen for the program. Goals color every other decision from curriculum to organization to staff training to scheduling to follow-up.

Yet no one set of goals is right for every congregation. No one can define the direction of a specific VBS except those to whom the ministry belongs. But someone in that congregation must define the direction. One would hope, however, that whatever the secondary goals, a fine balance will be struck between evangelism and teaching.

Establish Dates and Time

Once goals are stated, the next step is to determine when this VBS will be conducted—dates, time of day, and length. No one answer will be adequate for every situation.

When?

VBS may be scheduled at any time when children and youth are available to attend. Usually the best time is during the summer months when prospective students have relatively few activities scheduled. The preferred time during the summer is sometimes a matter of debate, but that decision will vary from church to church.

Some prefer an early summer VBS. They reason that children aren't yet out of the habit of attending school and studying, thus making it easier for VBS teachers. Weather is also milder in early June than it is later in the summer, at least in most parts of the country. In addition, summer school and community programs are not as likely to conflict. On the other hand, children may be tired of school, and some early summer community activities may conflict.

Other VBS leaders prefer to schedule their school in July. They reason that the children have been out of school long enough to enjoy the thought of returning to a school atmosphere. Early summer community programs may also be over. July, however, is a popular month for family vacations.

Still other leaders prefer VBS in August. They believe that it fills a void in the lives of restless children. The chief disadvantage is in scheduling planning and training meetings during vacations.

All things being equal, there is no one best time for VBS for all congregations. The selection of the dates should be based on data unique to each congregation. Determining factors include church camp schedule, community activities (baseball, swimming, summer school), congregational vacation patterns (often dependent upon shutdowns of local industries that employ large numbers of people), busy seasons for farmers, and local weather conditions. Each VBS leader needs to ascertain this information to the best of his or her ability, then make the decision, realizing of course, that no single date could be chosen that would avoid all conflicts. The goal is to avoid the major ones.

How Long?

How long should VBS last? The answer to that question also varies. Many churches still conduct a two-week school. Some have five days. Others have a morning and afternoon program for five days. Still others have eight days.

The eight-day program usually is done in one of three patterns: four days each week for two weeks (either Monday through Thursday or Tuesday through Friday), five days the first week and three the second (beginning on Wednesday and ending on Friday).

Some schools have also utilized the Sunday-school hour on the Sunday between the two weeks to include a ninth lesson.

Another possibility is to build a day-camp program—a day per week for ten weeks—and use the VBS materials for Bible lessons. This would be an excellent follow-up to the traditional VBS.

What Time of Day?

What hours to conduct the VBS program is another question. Morning? Afternoon? Evening? When is the best time?

There is no best time. It depends upon your purpose in having VBS in the first place, as well as circumstances in your community. If you conduct your program during the day, you will likely reach more unchurched children. If you have your program in the evening, you can include more youth and adults in the classes and make VBS a family affair. So define your purpose first, survey your community needs and patterns, then plan your VBS accordingly. Some churches plan some VBS classes for the morning and some for the evening, particularly when they are short of space. Use your imagination. Pick the best time for you.

Design an Effective Organization

The amount of organization needed for VBS is directly related to the size of the school. You need enough organization to get the job done—but no more. You need an organization with clear lines of communication, responsibility, and authority to do the job effectively. It is essential that this organizational plan be laid out before recruiting workers so that the leader knows exactly what he will need in terms of workers before he sets to work to get them.

Some guidelines should be kept in mind in deciding how many classes to plan. Recommendations for space, age grouping, class size, and teacher/pupil ratio should be followed as closely as possible in order to have as productive a VBS as possible. The goal is to provide personalized Bible teaching, not to exercise mob control. To do so requires careful planning. The chart below will serve as a handy reference.

Needed Space Per Pupil	Age	Ideal Class Size	Teacher/Pupil Ratio
30-35 sq. ft.	1	3-4	1/3
30-35 sq. ft.	2-3	4-5	1/4
30-35 sq. ft.	4-5	5-6	1/5
25-30 sq. ft.	Grades 1-2	6-7	1/6-7
25-30 sq. ft.	Grades 3-4	6-7	1/7
25-30 sq. ft.	Grades 5-6	7-8	1/8
20-25 sq. ft.	Grades 7-8	8-10	1/10
20-25 sq. ft.	Grades 9-12	12-15	1/15
15-18 sq. ft.	Adults	30-35	1/35

As you develop your organizational pattern, keep five simple principles in mind. To do so is to insure a more successful VBS.

1. Try to avoid having any volunteer supervisor directly supervise the work of more than six other people. That avoids diffusing the work of one supervisor among too many people.

17

2. Always have at least two workers in each class, especially the younger age groups.
3. Adhere as closely as possible to class sizes and teacher/pupil ratios.
4. Rearrange space assignments to meet space needs as they arise.
5. Clarify job responsibilities at the time of recruitment. Hand out printed sheets that summarize job responsibilities, or develop a handbook for use year after year. (See Chapter 4 for sample job descriptions.)

Armed now with size and space guidelines and organizational principles, the VBS leader must make a projection of possible VBS enrollment. Do that by examining records from last year, checking Sunday-school and youth-group attendance patterns, and adding 10 to 15 percent for those new pupils to be reached through evangelistic contacts. With that information in hand, decide how many classes and departments are needed.

Small VBS

In a small VBS of 50-75, the director can readily supervise all teachers himself. This author once worked in a VBS of fifty pupils. The organizational chart might have been drawn as follows:

VBS of 50

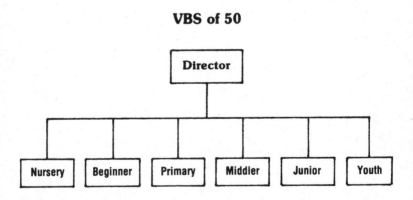

Medium-size VBS

As the size of the VBS increases, so must the organization that will support it, if it is to run smoothly. An effort must be made to spread out the responsibilities among more people. The coordinator of the VBS program (this could be the director of Christian education, youth minister, or volunteer VBS director) works with two or three others who supervise the activities of the specific age level. The coordinator and department supervisors meet together to plan recruitment procedures and other VBS policies and programs. Each is given a list of prospective workers for recruitment, presented with a set of guidelines under which to operate, assigned space, and given a general time schedule in which to plan the activities of the department. An organizational chart would look similar to the one below.

VBS of 150

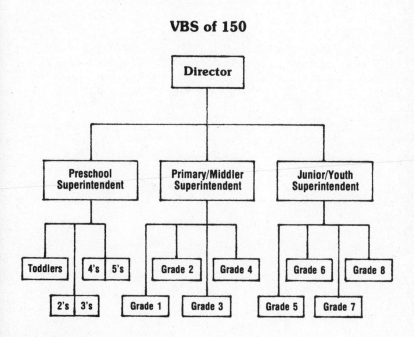

Large VBS

A yet larger program requires additional organization. Each age division may have its own director with department leaders working under that director. The age-level director is assigned a portion of the building and told to develop his own program within the guidelines established for the entire school. The director of Christian education and the age-level directors meet together to work out plans and policies affecting everyone and to develop a worker recruitment list. The director of Christian education may recruit transportation, kitchen, and publicity staff and work with them to acquaint them with their responsibilities.

19

The organizational chart for a school of this size might be pictured as follows:

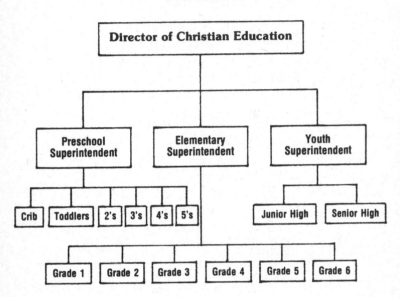

VBS of 300

Once the organization is outlined, the recruitment procedure can be readily planned and implemented. Until the outline is complete, however, it is difficult to visualize needed staffing.

Prepare a Planning Calendar

One last initial planning step is to develop a planning calendar that will pinpoint in advance when every job for VBS is to be done. Some publishers provide planning calendars for your adaptation and use. Your calendar should be completed in the planning stages for VBS so that adequate time is allowed for each task along the way and so that no important task is left undone. Each item can be checked off as it is completed, leaving the director confident of the smooth flow of the program. The sample calendar on the next page can be adapted to any VBS date.

as early as possible
____ Set goals.
____ Choose VBS dates and time.
____ Order a sample curriculum kit and filmstrip to review the course.
____ Outline organizational plans.
____ Pray. Seek guidance in assigning activities, recruiting workers, and ordering materials.

4 months before VBS (date) _____
____ Appoint department leaders.
____ Plan teacher development program.
____ Plan missions project. Contact missionary or organization related to the project.
____ Plan closing program.
____ Meet with department superintendents to discuss recruitment and planning and to communicate guidelines. Pray with them.

3 months before VBS (date) _____
____ Recruit staff.
____ Order lesson and craft materials. Use last year's records to guide your ordering.
____ Plan publicity campaign.

2 months before VBS (date) _____
____ Give materials to department superintendents.
____ Give materials to teachers.
____ Plan dedication service for VBS workers. Secure the minister's approval and assistance.
____ Conduct training program.
____ Plan for pre-registration.
____ Plan follow-up program.
____ Plan awards for contests.
____ Plan transportation.
____ Begin publicity (6 weeks before).

1 month before VBS (date) _____
____ Order all supplies not previously ordered.
____ Show VBS filmstrip to the entire congregation.
____ Continue publicity.
____ Recheck staff and materials.

___ Plan decorations.
___ Conduct pre-registration.
___ Check and adjust time schedules.
___ Continue training program.

immediately before VBS (date) _____
___ Hold final staff meeting.
___ Recheck all details.
___ Set up decorations.
___ Arrange classrooms.

during VBS (date) _____
___ Pray with and for your staff regularly.
___ Maintain spirit of enthusiasm and encourage workers.
___ Secure additional supplies as needed.
___ Visit departments; make necessary adjustments.
___ Have someone available to run errands.
___ Make sure secretarial records are being kept properly.
___ Direct the closing program.

after VBS (date) _____
___ Thank the Lord for His blessings.
___ Express appreciation to all workers.
___ Begin follow-up program. Visit the homes of all students who attended VBS.
___ See that supplies are sorted, packed, labeled, and stored for next year.
___ File names and addresses of workers to be contacted next year.
___ Make written notes of all good ideas for VBS next year. Note how problems were solved and how to avoid similar problems in the future.
___ Collect staff evaluations; tabulate them.
___ Make sure reports are completed. Include notes of necessary adjustments in schedules, additional supplies needed, etc.

Summary

Planning is never a waste of time. Once the initial decisions are made, VBS preparation can begin. With a carefully designed plan of action, a VBS director can proceed with the confidence that the program will be used to the glory of God.

Project

1. Interview leaders in your church and/or VBS to find out (1) how dates are selected, (2) what the goals for VBS are, and (3) how VBS has usually been organized and why.
2. Develop an organizational chart for the next VBS to be conducted in your congregation.

Bibliography

Getz, Gene. *The Vacation Bible School in the Local Church.* Chicago: Moody Press, 1962.

Self, Margaret (ed.). *How to Plan and Organize Year-Round Bible Ministries.* Glendale, CA: Gospel Light, 1976.

VBS: How-to-Do-It. Chicago: Scripture Press, 1956.

Chapter 3

SELECT CURRICULUM MATERIALS

As you read, think about the following:
1. What are the criteria by which curriculum materials are to be evaluated?
2. How can VBS materials be used beyond the VBS itself?
3. How should VBS materials be chosen?

One of the most important steps in preparing for VBS is to select the curriculum materials that will form the basis for Bible teaching in the VBS program. Many denominations and independent publishers produce VBS materials. Not every source of materials, however, is appropriate for every situation.

The director of the VBS should obtain preview kits from those curriculum sources in which he is interested just as soon as those kits are available (usually shortly after the first of the year). Then he and department leaders or a few key workers should evaluate the materials using acceptable criteria, like those presented later in this chapter, and keeping in mind the goals for the VBS program. They may also attend preview sessions at the local Christian bookstore to see crafts, visuals, and other tools. The final selection can then be made on the basis of this kind of objective data.

Criteria for Effective Curriculum

A comparative rating scale is a helpful device for comparing various curriculum sources. The scale included here covers the major areas of consideration.

Biblical Content
1. Pick one lesson at random from the materials for each department. Are the lessons Bible based? Is the purpose to teach the Word of God?

2. Check any doctrinal statements. What is said about the Bible? In the absence of a statement, look for lessons that present the deity of Christ, His miracles and resurrection. Do these lessons maintain a view of Scripture as the inerrant Word of God?
3. Pick a lesson at random from materials for each department. Are extrabiblical materials used correctly?
4. Survey two Middler and Junior lessons. Are salvation aims prominent? Is the gospel presented clearly and simply?
5. Check aims to locate lessons in different age groups that relate to Christian living or spiritual growth. Is the teaching clear and Biblical?
6. Are "spiritual tone" and a love for the Lord Jesus evident in the lessons?

Particular strengths and weaknesses of materials in specific departments:

Pedagogy
1. Is the teaching plan suitable for the age group?
2. Check to see that lessons for each department are planned for *teaching*. Do all elements of the program relate to the lesson aim?
3. Examine the music, games, learning activities, and crafts. Do they make a definite contribution to the teaching aim?
4. How are pupils' books used?
5. List all readiness (pre-session) activities suggested for all ages. Is a variety of activities suggested?

6. List methods suggested for in-class use. Is a variety of methods used? Are the methods pupil-centered rather than teacher-centered? List in-class methods.

7. Examine two Middler, Junior, and Youth lessons. Does the teacher's book suggest ways to get pupils to use their Bibles in class? Examine the pupils' books. Do they prompt and aid home study?

Particular strengths and weaknesses of materials in specific departments:

Pupil-Relatedness
1. Examine the aims for all lessons for each department. Are the aims stated in terms of what the pupil is to do as a result of his study? Are they related to the pupils' life-needs? How?

Study the application sections of two lessons in each department. Are the lesson aims carried out effectively? How?

2. Look through the lessons for each department. List the illustrations and applications given. Are these true to life? List the different needs of pupils in each department to which Bible truths are applied. Is there a variety of real-life problems—the kinds of problems pupils face each day? Do the materials, overall, seem "real life"?

3. Are the pupils' books graded to fit the developing skills of children and youth? Are there real differences in the kind and difficulty of exercises among the various books?
   Particular strengths and weaknesses of materials in specific departments:

Teachability
1. Check one lesson from each department. Are the lessons organized clearly, with step-by-step plans for teachers to follow?
2. Do the lessons give teachers how-to help, as well as suggesting what to teach?
3. Are correlated teaching aids available?

Particular strengths and weaknesses of materials in specific departments:

Attractiveness
1. Are the paper and binding of high quality?
2. Is the material well written?
3. Is the material attractive and readable (art, layout, type, style, etc.)?

Particular strengths and weaknesses of materials in specific departments:

Overall strengths and weaknesses of the materials:

Sources of VBS Materials

VBS materials may be obtained from several sources. Most publishers provide VBS planbooks that describe their courses and related products. A reference guide may be helpful to the VBS leader who needs to know pertinent information about curriculum producers. Although one source may be the accepted publisher for a church, other sources are valuable for use in day camps, camps, and other Bible teaching programs.

Publisher	N	B	P	M	J	Y	A	S	5-Day	10-Day
Augsburg 426 S. Fifth Minneapolis, MN 55415 (Lutheran)	X	X	X	X	X	X	X			X
Concordia 3558 S. Jefferson St. Louis, MO 63118 (Lutheran)	X	X	X	X	X	X	X	X	X	X
Cooperative Publication Association Box 179 St. Louis, MO 63166 (Twelve denominations)	X	X	X	X	X	X			X	X
Gospel Light Box 387 Ventura, CA 93006 (Non-denominational)	X	X	X	X	X	X	X		X	X

Publisher	Ages								Length	
	N	B	P	M	J	Y	A	S	5-Day	10-Day
Herald Press 616 Walnut Avenue Scottsdale, PA 15683 (Mennonite)	X	X	X	X	X	X	X		X	X
Regular Baptist Press 1300 N. Meacham Road Schaumberg, IL 60195 (Baptist)	X	X	X		X	X	X		X	X
Standard Publishing 8121 Hamilton Avenue Cincinnati, OH 45231 (Independent)	X	X	X	X	X	X	X	X	X	X
Sweet Publishing Company Box 4005 Austin, TX 78765 (Church of Christ)	X	X	X	X	X	X	X		X	X

N=Nursery, B=Beginner, P=Primary, M=Middler, J=Junior, Y=Youth, A=Adult, S=Special Education; Standard Publishing and Concordia provide materials for use with mentally retarded pupils.

SUMMARY

Curriculum materials are important for a successful VBS to achieve its goals. These should be selected on the basis of an objective evaluation of their merit.

Project
Evaluate at least one source of VBS material, using the criteria listed in this chapter.

Bibliography

Daniel, Eleanor; Gresham, Charles; and Wade, John. *Introduction to Christian Education.* Cincinnati: Standard Publishing, 1980.

Freese, Doris A. *Vacation Bible School.* Wheaton, IL: Evangelical Teacher Training Association, 1977.

Richards, Lawrence O. (ed.). *The Key to Sunday School Achievement.* Chicago: Moody Press, 1965.

Chapter 4

RECRUIT AND TRAIN WORKERS

As you read, think about the following:
1. What are the four basic steps in recruiting and training workers?
2. Why are job descriptions useful?
3. Where can workers for VBS be found?
4. How can workers be persuaded to help in VBS?
5. How should VBS workers be trained?

Recruitment and development of VBS personnel is hard work. But it is necessary work if VBS is to succeed. And it is rewarding work when personnel develop into able teachers and leaders. Yet it is work.

The importance of this aspect of VBS preparation cannot be overemphasized, for the outcome of the VBS program rests on the shoulders of those who teach and lead. The director alone cannot make a program succeed. But he can choose the right people to do the ministry of VBS. It is essential, then, to carefully implement this aspect of preparation.

Determine Needed Staff

Much of the planning work was done when the basic organizational pattern was projected in the initial planning phase. The number of classes and departments was outlined at that time.

There are other jobs to be done, however, and the number of people needed to do them is directly related to the number of classes and departments. List every job that needs to be done: music director, devotional leader, missions leader, department leaders, teachers, craft leaders, refreshment workers, recreation leaders, transportation workers, publicity planners, closing program personnel, purchasing agent, secretaries, etc. Then decide which jobs can be combined to be done by one person if it is necessary.

31

Write Job Guidelines

Decide exactly what each job is to entail so that the responsibility can be clearly communicated to would-be workers. It may be beneficial to write these so they can be distributed to the staff.

Written job descriptions need not be lengthy—in fact, they probably should be brief enough to avoid intimidating workers. But they should include exactly what is expected of each worker. Sample descriptions are included, although they will need to be altered or combined to meet needs in your congregation.

VBS Director
A. Responsible to elders (or Christian Education Committee)
B. Tasks
    1. Pray daily.
    2. Set goals for VBS.
    3. Outline needed organization.
    4. Develop a planning calendar or adapt the one provided by your publisher.
    5. Recruit department superintendents, craft director, and song leader **(4 months ahead)** from the approved list of workers. Clearly outline their responsibilities at the time of recruitment. Follow up by mailing a job description.
    6. Call superintendents' meetings and preside over them.
    7. Turn in curriculum order to purchasing chairman **(3 months ahead).**
    8. Plan the time schedule.
    9. Assign classroom areas.
    10. Organize and preside over training activities.
    11. Oversee daily staff devotions.
    12. Personally observe department programs during VBS.
    13. Supervise and participate in the closing program.
    14. Preside at the school evaluation meeting.
    15. Supervise the follow-up program.
    16. Be in charge of teacher appreciation activities.

Department Superintendent
A. Responsible to the VBS director
B. Tasks
    1. Pray daily.

2. Participate in superintendents' meetings as called by the VBS director.
3. Recruit teachers and co-workers for your department **(3 months ahead)** from the approved list provided you by the VBS director.
4. Clearly outline each person's job at the time of recruitment. Follow up with mailing a job description.
5. Lead department sessions at training activities.
6. Work closely with the VBS director in working out department problems.
7. Help teachers plan special features for their classes.
8. Give teacher paks to teachers **(2 months ahead).**
9. Obtain lists for special supplies from teachers and give to the purchasing chairman **(1 month ahead).** Pick up your department's supplies from the supply area before VBS begins. Sort and label supplies and place in the supply center on the final day of VBS.
10. Pick up enrollment/attendance cards and attendance forms from the VBS secretary the first day of VBS.
11. See that all rooms are ready for the opening day of VBS.
12. Arrive at least fifteen minutes early each day to participate in registration of new pupils. Encourage your staff to arrive early.
13. Preside at department assembly periods.
14. Pick up attendance cards and take to the secretary each day. Also take a count to the kitchen.
15. Keep your department on schedule.
16. Lead your department in an evaluation meeting.
17. Encourage each teacher and co-worker to make a home visit on each unchurched pupil in his class and to send a postcard to each church-related pupil.
18. Participate in the school evaluation.

Teacher
A. Responsible to the department superintendent
B. Tasks
1. Pray daily.
2. Participate in the training activities.
3. Prepare the lessons, visuals, and pupil book activities.
4. Plan special features for your class.
5. Turn in your list of special supplies to your superintendent **(1 month ahead).**
6. Obtain enrollment cards from your superintendent on the first day of VBS. Return them to your superintendent at the end of VBS.

7. Arrive at least fifteen minutes early each day to prepare your room and to pray.
8. Teach the Bible lesson each day.
9. Acquaint yourself with the crafts to be made each day and assist the co-worker during that time.
10. Lead in recreational activities, if necessary.
11. Sit with your pupils in all assemblies. Also stay with them during rest-room and refreshment time.
12. Participate with your pupils in the closing program.
13. Participate in an evaluation of your department.
14. With your co-worker, make a home visit on each unchurched pupil in your class and send a postcard to each church-related pupil within one month after VBS.

Teacher's Co-worker
A. Responsible to the teacher with whom you are working and the craft leader for your department
B. Tasks
1. Pray daily.
2. Participate in training activities.
3. Make a poster with your class identification on it so your pupils will know where to line up.
4. Serve as the teacher when the regular teacher must be absent.
5. Arrive at least fifteen minutes early in order to have your pupils lined up and ready to enter the building.
6. Check attendance cards at each session and put them outside your classroom door as soon as possible.
7. Lead your class in making the craft. (The craft leader for your department will demonstrate the crafts at a training session.)
8. Assist the teacher with other activities as needed. Be prepared to lead in a game during refreshment time, if time permits.
9. Sit with your pupils during assemblies. Also stay with your pupils during rest-room and refreshment time.
10. Participate in an evaluation of your department.
11. Participate with your pupils in the closing program.
12. Participate in the follow-up program with your teacher by making a home visit on each unchurched pupil in your class and by sending a postcard to each church-related pupil within one month after VBS.

Craft Director
A. Responsible to the VBS director

B. Tasks
1. Pray daily.
2. Select crafts and correlate them with the lessons.
3. Recruit a craft leader for each department **(3 months ahead)** from the approved list provided you by the VBS director. Clearly outline the craft leader's job at the time of recruitment. Follow up by mailing a job description.
4. Meet with craft leaders as many times as needed to work on the crafts.
5. Have all craft items purchased **(8 weeks ahead)** and bills turned in to the purchasing chairman. The VBS director will give you a budget.
6. Prepare your craft leaders to demonstrate the construction of crafts to their departments, display completed crafts, and tell how crafts correlate with the lessons when they lead in the craft training session.
7. Participate in training activities.
8. Be present during VBS to assist with crafts.
9. Participate in the school evaluation.
10. Store any unassembled craft projects immediately after VBS.

Craft Leader
A. Responsible to craft director
B. Tasks
1. Pray daily.
2. Participate in all meetings called by the craft director to work on crafts.
3. During the craft training session, demonstrate the construction of the crafts and display completed projects for your assigned department. Tell how the crafts correlate with the lessons.
4. Assist the craft director in the organization of craft materials.
5. Be present during VBS to assist your department with crafts.
6. Participate in your department evaluation.
7. Assist the craft director in storing unassembled craft projects immediately after VBS.

Song Leaders
A. Responsible to the VBS director (or department superintendent, if department assemblies are conducted)

B. Tasks
1. Pray daily.
2. Select and learn all songs that will be used during VBS **(at least one month ahead).** Correlate the songs with the daily lessons.
3. Give a list of all songs and music to the pianist **(one month ahead).**
4. At the training sessions, teach the theme song and other new songs to be used during VBS.
5. During the month preceding VBS, make arrangements with the superintendents of the children's Sunday-school departments to teach the VBS theme song, and other selected songs if time permits.
6. Lead daily song sessions during VBS.
7. Work with the director in planning the music for the closing program.
8. Lead the music for the closing program.
9. Participate in the school evaluation.

Pianists
A. Responsible to the song leader
B. Tasks
1. Pray daily.
2. Learn all VBS music **(2 weeks ahead)** from the list given you by the song leader.
3. Play for Sunday-school departments during the month preceding VBS as arranged by the song leader.
4. Play for the song session at training activities.
5. Play for the daily song sessions during VBS.
6. Participate in the school evaluation.

Secretary
A. Responsible to the VBS director
B. Tasks
1. Pray daily.
2. Recruit pre-registration committee members **(2 months ahead)** from the approved list provided you.
3. Work with your committee in planning and carrying out pre-registration activities.
   a. Set up a display table for pre-registration during the month preceding VBS.
   b. Place enrollment cards in the pew racks during the month preceding VBS.
   c. Have your committee sort the enrollment cards by age or grade just completed.

d. Give the enrollment cards and attendance forms to the department superintendents.
4. Arrive thirty minutes early during VBS to begin your secretarial duties.
   a. Set up tables for registration.
   b. Enroll new students as they arrive each day.
   c. Count the offering each day and record the amount.
   d. Deposit money daily.
   e. Make daily entries in the record forms.
   f. Announce attendance and offering statistics daily.
5. Lead your committee in an evaluation meeting.
6. Participate in the school evaluation.

Purchasing Chairman
A. Responsible to the VBS director
B. Tasks
1. Pray daily.
2. Keep a current report available.
3. Turn in all bills to the VBS director.
   a. Obtain curriculum materials order from the director and place the order **(10 weeks ahead).**
   b. Obtain publicity aids order from publicity chairman and place order **(7 weeks ahead).**
   c. Obtain bills for craft items from the craft director by beginning of VBS.
   d. Obtain supply lists from superintendents **(1 month ahead)** and purchase special supplies before VBS.
   e. Check supply of glue, pencils, construction paper, scissors, crayons, masking and cellophane tape, etc., and purchase necessary items.
   f. Obtain bills from the kitchen chairman by the close of VBS.
   g. Obtain closing program costs from the VBS director by the close of VBS.
4. Participate in the school evaluation.

Publicity Chairman
A. Responsible to the VBS director
B. Tasks
1. Pray daily.
2. Recruit publicity committee members **(8 weeks ahead)** from the approved lists provided you.
3. Lead your committee in planning the publicity campaign for VBS **(7 weeks ahead).**

4. Give your publicity-aids order to the purchasing chairman **(7 weeks ahead).**
5. Begin major publicity campaign **(at least 6 weeks ahead).**
6. Participate in the school evaluation.

Kitchen Chairman
A. Responsible to the VBS director
B. Tasks
   1. Pray daily.
   2. Recruit kitchen committee members **(1 month ahead)** from the approved list supplied you.
   3. Obtain and serve food for special events, as requested.
      a. Training sessions
      b. Closing program
      c. Other (evaluation meetings, etc.)
   4. Obtain and serve refreshments each day of VBS.
      a. Purchase needed supplies.
      b. Solicit items that can be donated.
         (1) Send sign-up sheet for donations to adult Sunday-school classes during month preceding VBS.
         (2) Put a sign-up sheet for donations on the bulletin board during month preceding VBS.
   5. Turn in bills to the purchasing chairman by the end of VBS.
   6. Supervise the kitchen committee in serving and cleanup.
   7. Lead your committee in an evaluation meeting.
   8. Participate in the school evaluation.

Transportation Chairman
A. Responsible to VBS director
B. Tasks
   1. Pray daily.
   2. Recruit a bus driver from the approved list provided you.
   3. Recruit a bus captain from the approved list provided you.
   4. Obtain list of persons needing rides from the VBS director before the first day of VBS.
   5. Develop a bus schedule to be publicized before VBS begins.
   6. Arrive early and have the bus captain arrive at least fifteen minutes before bus departure time.

7. See that the bus departs on schedule.
8. When the bus arrives at the church building, have the bus captain help registered pupils find their class lines. You will take unregistered pupils to the appropriate registration area.
9. See that the bus is cleaned out each day.
10. Participate in the school evaluation.

determined staff needs

Recruiting VBS Workers

sources

Start the recruitment procedure by making a list of the staff for the past several years. It is important to go back beyond the previous year to avoid missing someone who can and will help under ordinary circumstances. Make sure you note what job each person completed when he worked before.

The Sunday-school teaching roster is also a good starting place for VBS recruitment. New workers who have not previously worked in VBS are often added to the Sunday-school staff during the year. Make sure you find out where they work.

New members who haven't yet assumed responsibility for teaching offer good possibilities for the VBS staff. Many newcomers from other congregations may have teaching experience that should be tapped. New Christians may also be willing to assist in some way.

College students are a fourth source of workers. They will be enthusiastic additions to the staff, if they can arrange VBS into their work schedules. High-school students also do good work in positions where they don't have to assume full responsibility and when they are adequately supervised. (Some are mature enough to work by themselves—but be sure that they have proved themselves first before thrusting too much responsibility upon them.)

Each prospective worker should be contacted personally, either by phone or with a personal call. A telephone call is probably adequate to reconfirm previous VBS workers unless there is some particular problem to be considered. Recruitment of new workers suggests a personal call to explain the VBS ministry and the nature of the job for which the person is being recruited.

A simple recruitment form will help to organize this task. In fact, your VBS publisher may have such forms available for purchase. The one below is a sample. Completed forms may be saved from one year to the next to assist the next director in developing a list of prospective workers.

Survey

prospect list

match prospects w/ jobs they are interested in + qualified for

You have made decisions about what job to suggest to each person when you contact them

Name:		
Address: _____ Telephone: _____		
Contacted: _____ by _____		
Will ☐ will not ☐ work. Why? _____		

Dept. Supt.		Secretary		Provide Cookies	
Teacher		Kitchen		Transportation	
Co-Worker		Storyteller		Address Mailings	
Craft Leader		Puppets		Cut Out Visuals	
Recreation		Missions		Other:	
Song Leader		Publicity			
Pianist		Purchasing			

This form can be distributed in the church paper and Sunday bulletin a week or two before recruitment is to begin. The results will save time and get the recruitment drive off to a good start.

Develop Workers

Staff training to prepare workers for VBS ministry must be carefully planned. Some churches conduct a series of special VBS meetings to provide training and to permit group planning. Others leave training up to department leaders with only one or two general staff meetings.

The nature of staff training must be determined by the needs of the staff members. If the staff is composed mainly of veteran workers, who already possess effective teaching skills, a review/planning session or two may be adequate. On the other hand, inexperienced workers require more training time. The director's guide included with the curriculum, as well as the teacher's books, include a variety of suggestions and step-by-step guidelines. These may be modified to meet local needs.

Some training sessions should be general sessions for all workers. These times are used to develop staff morale, inform workers of pertinent information (space, dates, supplies, missions, etc.), introduce the curriculum, and learn music. One or two general sessions should be adequate.

40

Most sessions, however, should be departmental in nature, in which practical, curriculum-related training is done. Topics that may be covered in these sessions are age-level characteristics, discipline, use of various learning activities included in the lessons, crafts, scheduling, lesson planning, use of visuals, using materials creatively, the learning process, follow-up, teaching methods, and use of memory work. Department responsibilities should also be assigned during these sessions. Two to five sessions would be profitable to workers.

VBS training sessions may be conducted as separate sessions of sixty to ninety minutes. However, some churches have found success with one four- to six-hour training session. An hour of this session is spent in a general assembly, the remainder in departmental sessions where training is done, crafts are displayed and explained, and music is learned.

role play

Recruit me

✓ new member transfer

✓ husband at home
dying of cancer

Summary

pregnant
w/ 5th

Recruitment and training is work, but work that can be readily managed if it is carefully outlined. Needs must be determined, jobs described, people contacted, and staff trained. When recruitment is completed at least two months before VBS begins, and when training is done at least a month in advance, the VBS program will be successful.

grandma
moved in
last we

Projects

1. Write a job description for at least two positions in your VBS.
2. Plan a department training session that is age-related, curriculum-related, and practical. Use the age level of your choice.

7. Give support +
help letter
materials

Bibliography

Daniel, Eleanor; Gresham, Charles; and Wade, John. *Introduction to Christian Education.* Cincinnati: Standard Publishing, 1980.
Gangel, Kenneth O. *Leadership for Church Education.* Chicago: Moody Press, 1970.

training
prayer

Complete 90
days before
VBS

3 Provide prospect w/ info
dates
time   *tch tr. dates*
job descr

1 Be positive in your approach. I would like you to think about
2 Ask if they would help as a ___
4. I will call you on ___ (within a wk)
5. Pray for them
6. Call back on apppt date   *if yes answer 3. if no thank them for considering*

pray 41 *a ministry opportunity throu VBS*

Chapter 5

PLAN A WORKABLE
TIME SCHEDULE

As you read, think about the following:
1. What activities should be included in the VBS schedule?
2. What guidelines will help to plan a worship service?
3. What are some other expressional activities in addition to crafts?
4. What guidelines will help to design a schedule for each age level?
5. How can the VBS be scheduled for various ages?

A workable daily time schedule makes it possible for VBS to achieve its objectives. Every activity of the day should be designed to accomplish the learning goals for that day. The business of developing a workable schedule depends upon (1) the goals of the school, (2) the activities that are designed to accomplish the goals, (3) the age level for which it is designed, and (4) the facilities in which the VBS is conducted. This section will present the components to be included, tips for various age levels, and sample schedules.

Activities That Teach

Worship
An important part of the VBS program is worship, that time when the pupils gather to sing praises to God. It is an essential time for creating a group spirit and to direct attention toward God. Some churches include a devotional thought or the missions presentation during this time.

Worship should be a natural response to God's Word—a time of adoration and praise. This may have some affect as to *where* it is placed in the schedule. Many leaders are rethinking where it fits best and have, therefore, moved it to the end of the session. Then the music and activities can reinforce the

Bible truths already learned. (This should be true whether the assembly is conducted first, last, or in the middle.)

It is probably best not to plan a worship service for everyone in the VBS at the same time in the same place. The most important reason is that not all age levels have the same length of attention span nor do they worship in the same way. Preschoolers need shorter formal worship times than do older children. In addition, graded worship times permit the selection of songs most suitable to the age level in terms of words, range, and rhythm.

The large VBS may have several departmental worship times. Smaller schools may conduct two or three worship sessions. Even the small school of fifty or less would profit from conducting a preschool worship time and one for older children.

Bible Study

An adequate amount of time should be included for Bible study, for it is one of the major activities of the school. The required amount of time varies from age level to age level, although most VBS materials could profitably be used in a one-hour time segment for any age level by the time learning centers, Bible information, and life applications are developed. This one-hour time segment could also include the assembly time for younger children.

The VBS leader should carefully analyze the amount of time that is given to the study of the Word of God. This should never be whittled down to allow time for other activities, as good as they may be.

Crafts and Expressional Time

Crafts are as "VBS" as apple pie and hot dogs are "American." But these should be chosen to contribute to the VBS goals, and they should never overshadow Bible study.

A director of crafts can help to correlate the craft program with the lesson objectives. Such a person should have a deep concern for Bible teaching and should, at the same time, be creative enough to plan craft projects to carry out the Bible teaching. He can recruit and train a staff to do Bible teaching through crafts.

It may be an advantage to use the packaged crafts available from the publisher. Those crafts have been planned, designed, and produced with Bible teachings as the foremost objective. Creativity, uniqueness, and practicality are considered as well. Packaged crafts save hours of planning for correlation, shopping for materials, and training of staff. When you consider every cost, they may also be more economical.

Actually, expressional activity time need not be confined only to crafts. A variety of activities could be chosen: music, puppets, drama, work around the church building for older pupils, or making furniture and toys to be used in the children's teaching program, to name a few examples. These activities can readily work with material that fits in with overall VBS goals.

Some churches have used a VBS Store idea for expressional time. The pupils are assigned curriculum-related tasks, such as memory work, papers, and application projects, each of which carries a monetary value (this expressed in VBS dollars). The expressional time is used for pupils to report their progress, exchange their learning tasks for VBS dollars, and visit the VBS Store where they can exchange their "money" for pictures, posters, books, and other items that have been priced in VBS dollars.

Recreation and Refreshments

A break time needs to be planned into the VBS schedule to provide a change of pace in activities. This need not be long—probably it should not be—but the pupils do need a chance to move about and get rid of their wiggles. Make every effort to choose activities that correlate with the lesson goals for the day.

Age-Level Consideration

The daily schedule need not be the same for every age level or even for every department. Some components may have to be in common, e.g., worship if there is a combined worship time. Or some aspects may have to be done at specific times for specific age levels because of the need to make multiple use of an auditorium, playground, or assembly room. These can be taken into account and still permit development of a tailor-made schedule for each age division.

Preschool

Preschool children would do well to go directly to their classrooms and begin immediate involvement in learning activities designed to teach the Bible truth for the day. Bible story times need to be comparatively short. Worship times work best toward the middle of the session after the child has already been involved in meaningful Bible learning activities.

Adequate craft time must be allotted so that the child can do his work himself.

Elementary

Elementary children also respond well when they can go immediately to their classrooms to become involved in meaningful Bible learning activities to develop the Bible theme for the day. Although it is possible to have children do this, then break for an opening assembly, such a plan is disruptive to a smooth flow of time and efficient use of time. It is preferable to develop the Bible teaching session first, then have worship and the remaining elements of the program.

Youth

On the other hand, youth have a hunger for fellowship. They want to talk to each other—and they do whether you have planned for it or not. So plan in a time of fellowship at the very beginning. Worship may be better planned at the end of the session for youth as well as for other ages.

Sample Schedules

No one schedule can meet the needs for every VBS, of course, for each situation must take into account facilities, available pianists and song leaders, and special goals and/or needs to be met. However, using the elements of VBS mentioned and taking into account special age considerations, schedules may be similar to the ones below.

Early Childhood

(Toddlers-Kindergarten)

	2½ hours	2 hours
Bible Learning Activities .... (Learning Centers)	40 minutes	35 minutes
Assembly Time .... (Worship and Missions)	30 minutes	25 minutes
Recreation and Refreshments ..	20 minutes	15 minutes
Bible Story and Pupil Books	20 minutes	15 minutes
Crafts	35 minutes	25 minutes
Clean-Up Time	5 minutes	5 minutes

Elementary Children

(Grades 1-6)

	2½ hours	2 hours
Bible Study	65 minutes	50 minutes
(Learning Centers, Bible Information, Application)		
Assembly Time	30 minutes	30 minutes
(Worship and Missions)		
Recreation and Refreshments ..	20 minutes	15 minutes
Crafts	35 minutes	25 minutes

Youth

(Grades 7-12)

	2½ hours	2 hours
Fellowship Time	10 minutes	10 minutes
Bible Study/Bible Application ...	65 minutes	50 minutes
Crafts and Refreshments	40 minutes	30 minutes
Worship and Missions	35 minutes	30 minutes

Adults

	2½ hours	2 hours
Fellowship Time	10 minutes	10 minutes
Bible Study I	65 minutes	50 minutes
Refreshments	10 minutes	10 minutes
Bible Study II	65 minutes	50 minutes

(If you choose to use crafts for adults, you may lengthen Bible Study I by ten to fifteen minutes, then allot the remaining time from Bible Study II to the crafts.)

Summary

Designing an effective schedule is a matter of knowing what components to include in a program, heeding special age considerations, then designing a schedule that takes into account both items plus the goals for VBS. No one way is best for every situation. But the principles apply in every circumstance.

Project

For each age level in your VBS, design a schedule that will take into account the principles outlined in this chapter plus the special circumstances of your congregation. How does your end product compare to or differ from the sample schedules presented in this chapter? Why?

Bibliography

Daniel, Eleanor; Gresham, Charles; and Wade, John. *Introduction to Christian Education.* Cincinnati: Standard Publishing, 1980.

Getz, Gene. *The Vacation Bible School in the Local Church.* Chicago: Moody Press, 1962.

Bolton, Barbara, and Smith, Charles. *Creative Bible Learning for Children: Grades 1-6.* Glendale, CA: ICL, 1977.

Harrell, Donna, and Haystead, Wesley. *Creative Bible Learning for Young Children: Birth to 5 Years.* Glendale, CA: ICL, 1977.

Marlowe, Monroe, and Reed, Bobbie. *Creative Bible Learning for Adults.* Glendale, CA: ICL, 1977.

Reed, Ed, and Reed, Bobbie. *Creative Bible Learning for Youth: Grades 7-12.* Glendale, CA: ICL, 1977.

Self, Margaret (ed.) *How to Plan and Organize Year-Round Bible Ministries.* Glendale, CA: Gospel Light, 1976.

Chapter 6

PUBLICIZE!

As you read, think about the following:
1. Who is responsible for VBS promotion?
2. List four basic principles for effective VBS promotion.
3. What are four types of VBS promotion? Give examples of
   each.

It is one thing to have VBS planned and ready to go, but it is
yet another to let people know that you are having it. Imagine
prepared teachers in their places with no pupils. Suppose for
a moment that goals have been carefully defined, but someone has failed to let people know they were invited to attend
the sessions. It sounds ludicrous, but unfortunately it is often
the case.

Once a person has gone to all of the work to develop an
excellent VBS, he most surely wants people to come. But they
do not come if they do not know they are invited to come.
That is why good publicity is so critical.

Plan for Publicity

Good promotion is so much a part of conducting a successful VBS that it requires someone designated to plan and develop the publicity program. Publicity must never "just happen"; it must be directed toward particular target groups and
repeated if it is to have *measurable* value.

A publicity chairman, appointed to carry out the tasks iden-
tified in the job description in Chapter 4, can select a committee who will plan and implement a promotional program that
informs the target group of what VBS is and for whom it is
intended. Committee members may be people who cannot
serve during VBS and those who have a special interest in
and flair for promotional work. The size of the committee will
vary according to need and available people to be on it.

The committee plans a publicity program in keeping with

the goals of the school. They then submit the program to the director for approval and for allocation of funds.

A good publicity program begins early and outlines week-by-week activities to promote VBS. Methods will vary according to the target groups and available resources. But the task is to let the congregation and community know about VBS.

Publicity Principles

Good promotion is not so dependent upon novelty as it is upon thoroughness and persistance. Recognition of four basic promotional principles and careful implementation of them will provide the basis needed for effective communication.

1. *Know to whom you want to appeal.* Objectives determine the potential VBS audience. If the goal is primarily Bible teaching, the target audience is those within the congregation. If the goal is evangelistic, then a second audience is the community. If the goal is family emphasis, then adults also become a target group.

2. *Know what appeals to what group.* Certain themes appeal to adults, others to children or youth. The same is true for any target group. Before actual methods are selected, consensus must be reached about what to communicate to whom.

3. *Select methods to appeal to the target groups.* All possible media should be considered, then accepted or rejected on the basis of budget and other resources. Whatever is used should be of excellent quality in writing style, photography, art, and graphics. This need not be professional work, but it should be attractive, neat, and informative, a credit to the church from which it comes and the Lord whom it represents.

4. *Pray.* Ask God to bless the work done for promoting VBS.

Types of Promotion

Church Publicity

It is not a safe assumption that everybody within the congregation will know that VBS is coming, for some will miss its advent. Use every available device to inform the congregation about VBS.

- Hold a treasure hunt with a clue each Sunday. The last clue is available the first day of VBS. That will encourage first-day attendance.
- Have a VBS pre-registration fair. Set up fair booths with games. Each student who comes to pre-register for VBS is given tickets to visit each booth. Serve refreshments.
- Have a VBS clown who appears in Sunday-school classes before VBS begins. Perhaps he can also appear occasionally during VBS.
- Show a videotape from last year's VBS.
- Have a coloring contest among Sunday-school children.
- Teach VBS fingerplays in appropriate departments.
- Have a VBS preview night in which crafts are shown and music is learned.
- Show the VBS filmstrip in an evening service.
- Give VBS hats to children who pre-register.

- Recruit VBS prayer partners. Ask them to pray for specific children and workers who will be involved in the VBS program. Keep prayer partners informed of needs and progress both in the days before VBS and after the program concludes.
- Visit each adult Sunday-school class several weeks before VBS. Ask the members to supply the names of children who should attend VBS. Encourage them to bring those children to VBS.
- Show slides from previous VBS during an evening service.
- Teach the theme song in an evening service and in Sunday-school department assemblies.
- Prepare a mystery door in a well-traveled area of the building. It should be decorated and have a VBS message on the inside that can be read when the door is opened.

Other ideas:
- Catchy appeal announcements in the bulletin and church paper—Use art work when it is possible.

- Bulletin-board displays
- Testimonials by previous VBS workers in public assemblies of the congregation
- Testimonials by previous VBS students
- Hymnbook inserts to advertise VBS needs and/or dates
- Posters—either prepared commercially or entered in a poster contest among children of the congregation
- Lawn banner

- VBS interest centers in department assembly areas
- Peepboxes with a VBS message
- Worker-dedication service
- Pre-VBS contest to sign up unchurched pupils
- T-shirts given to all who pre-register
- Pre-registration days
- Picture albums from previous VBS programs displayed in Sunday-school departments
- Balloon launch with a VBS message to be returned by the finder to the sender
- Puppet program in Sunday school and children's church
- Skits in Sunday school and children's church
- Made-up crafts displayed in Sunday-school departments

Mailings
- VBS announcements stamped on all outgoing mail
- Postcards or "Come to VBS!" booklets to all of last year's enrollees
- Direct invitations to specific individuals
- Bulk mailings to a zip code area
- Church paper

Community Penetration
- Tickets to be distributed to neighborhood children
- Newspaper releases
- Paid newspaper advertising

- Community service announcements on radio and television
- Paid radio and television in places of business
- Posters in businesses
- Neighborhood distribution of individual flyers or "Come to VBS!" booklets

Personal Contacts
- Personal invitations. Prepare lists of pupils who attended VBS last year. Arrange the lists by classes. Give the lists to the appropriate teachers. Have each teacher send each person a postcard before VBS begins. Then have each teacher call each person a couple of days before VBS begins.
- Home calls
- Telephone chain

Summary

Publicity need not be flashy and unusual to be effective, but it must be thorough and repetitive. A good publicity committee will clearly identify the target groups, find out what appeals to them, and then set about providing materials that inform and build enthusiasm for VBS. Check the VBS Planbook from your publisher for a variety of tools and ideas.

Church publicity, mailings, community penetration, and personal contacts are all valid types of promotion. Each target group probably should be touched by more than one type of message.

Publicity, like every other phase of VBS ministry, must be planned carefully. But the possibilities abound, and the potential results are well worth the effort.

Project
1. Plan a promotion program for your church to appeal to unchurched children.
2. Develop a promotion to enroll adults in VBS.
3. Plan a VBS promotion program to reach church children who have been lethargic about attending VBS.

Bibliography
Cox, William (ed). *Ideas for VBS Promotion.* Nashville: Convention Press, 1973.

Freese, Doris A. *Vacation Bible School.* Wheaton, IL: Evangelical Teacher Training Association, 1977.

Hall, Arlene S. *Your Vacation Bible School.* Anderson, IN: Warner Press, 1956.

Chapter 7

BUILD A CLOSING PROGRAM

As you read, think about the following:
1. What are some possible closing activities for VBS?
2. List the guidelines for planning a closing program.
3. What types of closing programs can be developed?

The closing part of VBS should be as enthusiastic as the beginning. That will happen only when careful planning is made so that the closing activities and the closing program are the climax of the whole VBS effort.

Closing Activities

A special activity at the close of VBS is one way to maintain the good results of the teaching program. This can be an activity in which all pupils participate, or it can be several activities, one for each age level.

Some churches plan an end-of-school picnic either on the last day of VBS or on Saturday following the close of VBS. It is an exciting time, especially for younger children. In a large VBS, it may be best to have several department picnics with games and activities designed for that age group.

A picnic can be held on the church lawn, at a nearby park, or on an accessible farm. It need not be elaborate—sack lunches will do quite nicely—though the children would enjoy hot dogs and potato chips or fried chicken and potato salad. The key is simply to make it a special activity for all children and youth who have been in VBS.

Other churches plan field trips for older groups, perhaps to a synagogue or other points of interest associated with the Bible lessons. This kind of activity is usually reserved for Juniors and Youth with younger ages having a picnic.

A VBS Carnival or VBS Fair could work well for an end-of-school activity just as well as it could for a publicity event. This could also be combined with a picnic.

Closing Demonstration Program

The closing demonstration program provides opportunity to demonstrate to parents and church members what has been accomplished during VBS. It is a means whereby unchurched parents can come to the church building to hear a simple presentation of the gospel and to meet Christians who care for their children.

The closing program need not be elaborate. In fact, it should be simple enough that it requires relatively little rehearsal time. It should be a reflection of what has happened during VBS.

When should the closing program be held? Some churches conduct it during the final VBS session. However, this prohibits working mothers and fathers from attending if the VBS is conducted during the day. It also takes away one entire teaching session. Others, those who have morning schools, sometimes have it on the evening of the last day of VBS, a workable option. Some have it during Sunday school the Sunday after VBS is over. However, this generally is not the best time to attract unchurched pupils and parents to attend. Still others have their closing program at the evening service on the Sunday after VBS is over. Each church should choose the best time for it.

Program Tips

Several guidelines will be invaluable in planning an effective closing program. These should be carefully heeded.

1. Plan early—prior to VBS—and communicate the plans to the staff.
2. Plan a program that will last no longer than seventy-five minutes—keep it to sixty minutes if at all possible.
3. Use all pupils in the program (with the possible exception of high school youth) if only in a group presentation.
4. Distribute diplomas the last day of VBS. To do so in the closing program requires too much time.
5. Send out special invitations to parents to attend the program.
6. Reserve seats for VBS pupils.
7. Use youth to usher and receive offering. (This is a good job for high school youth.)
8. Plan what to do with preschool children after their presentation. Either have them return to their classrooms with their teachers or have them sit with their parents for the duration of the program.
9. Explain the purpose for the offering.

10. Recognize workers. Print names in a bulletin instead of naming each person.
11. Start and end the program on time.
12. Include a few minutes in the program for the minister to share with the audience.

Types of Programs

Four basic types of programming may be used for a closing program. Some elements of each could be included to produce a fifth type of program.

A unified program is one that centers around one theme. It should involve everyone who will contribute a facet of the theme. The directors' book from most publishers includes a unified program. This program will help provide an overview of daily themes emphasized during VBS.

A departmental program is a second option. Each department may present a short program of its own with no particular effort made to unify the various presentations. Teachers' books often include suggestions for such a program.

A third type of program is to reenact a day in VBS. Follow the schedule for a typical day of VBS. Give parents and visitors directions about where to go for classes and various activities. Allow them to move from place to place if they have several children in VBS. Conclude with a unified devotional service.

The fourth option is to develop the sights and sounds of VBS. Have someone take slides of highlights in the daily programs during VBS. Show these at the closing program complete with singing and narration by the pupils.

A sample closing program for one VBS combined several of these features. The format was:

Meet in Rooms .... 6:45 p.m.
Processional and Theme Song .... 7:00 p.m.
Preschool Musical Presentation .... 7:05 p.m.
Grades 1-3 Musical Presentation .... 7:10 p.m.
Grades 4-8 Musical Presentation .... 7:15 p.m.
Sights and Sounds of VBS .... 7:25 p.m.
Youth Drama Presentation .... 7:35 p.m.
Recognition of Workers .... 7:45 p.m.
Missions Presentation .... 7:46 p.m.
Minister's Minutes .... 7:56 p.m.
Closing Prayer .... 8:00 p.m.
Refreshments and Fellowship

Choose your closing program to give variety to what has been done before. The same type of program year after year elicits poor response. Plan to meet the needs and interests of your own congregation. For example, one church in Oregon planned an all-church picnic just prior to their VBS closing program. Whatever kind of program is chosen, review the VBS themes, display the crafts, and plan a short fellowship time with refreshments after the program itself.

Summary

Closing activities should be carefully planned to build upon the enthusiasm already experienced in VBS. Special activities for the pupils, such as picnics and field trips, are excellent.

The closing demonstration program should be a simple presentation to parents and other church members of the themes and the results of the VBS sessions. If it is carefully planned, it can be the right kind of climax for a special teaching ministry.

Project
Plan a closing program for your VBS. Choose one of the formats suggested in the chapter and develop in detail what you will do.

Bibliography
Getz, Gene. *The Vacation Bible School in the Local Church.* Chicago: Moody Press, 1962.

Mills, Linda. "Change of Pace Closing Program." *KEY to Christian Education.* Cincinnati: Standard Publishing, Fall, 1980.

Chapter 8

CONSERVE THE VBS IMPACT

As you read, think about the following:
1. Why is follow-up important in VBS?
2. What five areas of follow-up should be completed?
3. List follow-up activities in each area.

VBS ministry can—and should—be a year-long activity. Of course this does not mean that VBS sessions are conducted every week of the year nor that all workers are on duty all year. But the planning, implementation, and follow-up of VBS extend throughout the year.

Many VBS ministries stop when the last class is conducted. But if VBS is to achieve its greatest potential, an aggressive follow-up program must be initiated to preserve the gains made with pupils and workers. This aspect of the program should be no less carefully planned than publicity, class sessions, or staff development. Several areas of follow-up should be pursued.

Follow Up With Materials

Seldom do purchasers figure exactly the needs for supplies and materials for VBS. There are usually leftover teachers' books, pupils' books, supplies, and/or craft items. These items should be collected and stored for future use or returned to the supplier for credit.

Teachers' books, visual packets, assembly and mission materials, and VBS songbooks may be stored for reuse in later church programs. They make excellent graded worship or weekday curriculum. If this is the intent, they should be collected, sorted, filed, and placed in a media center or library where teachers can get to them. Another possibility is to collect teachers' books, visual packets, and partially used pupils' books for distribution to an English-speaking mission or to a new congregation. Whatever the choice, these materials need to be removed from classrooms.

Unused pupils' books can usually be returned to the VBS supplier for credit to the church account. The same is true of unopened craft materials. Careful attention to this can save several dollars of VBS expense. These could be stored for later use, however, if that choice is made for teachers' books.

Items such as scissors, crayons, craft sticks, and glue should be sorted and returned to classrooms or stored for future use in VBS. All equipment such as tables, chairs, flannelboards, and bulletin boards should be returned to where they were found.

A helpful device for future programs is to place an inventory of supplies and equipment, used and leftover, in the general records. Such a list eliminates much guesswork the next time.

Follow Up With Records

All records should be completed before VBS is considered over. This is an essential step if the proper follow-up ministry is developed for those who were enrolled.

Registration cards need to be fully completed with all pertinent information, especially the data regarding church preference. These cards may be filed or otherwise preserved for next year's publicity campaign. Names of all newly contacted families should be given to the minister and evangelistic callers so that contact can be made with each home.

The general record folder and/or book should be completed with pupils' names and data, staff names and assignments, curriculum, financial records, ordering information, surplus materials inventory, and evaluations. Include evaluative and explanatory notations for each section. Then file the material for use next year.

Finally, information reports need to be written and submitted to the proper groups. The Christian Education Committee, the church board, and the elders are likely recipients of these reports. Pertinent data from the reports should be published in the church paper.

Follow Up With Pupils

If VBS has developed as planned, new contacts will have been made. New interest will be evident, and renewed commitments may have been made. These must not be left without nurture.

The possibilities for follow-up are extensive as the following list indicates. No congregation should do all of these activities, but every one should probably do some of them.

• *Call on each pupil.* Teachers and other callers can be recruited to talk with each child and his parents. Instruct the callers to encourage each family to become involved in the regular church program.

• *Cultivate non-Christian homes.* This can be done through the regular evangelistic calling program.

• *Day camp.* Choose one day a week for an all-day program of recreation and study. The next chapter develops this idea in more detail.

• *Weekly club program.* Middlers, Juniors, and Youth respond well to weekday clubs. One Illinois church involved Middlers and Juniors in a study/choir program. An Indiana church had a bike-hikers club for Youth. Clubs could be developed around any number of interests—crafts, music, athletics, recreation, photography—whatever appeals to your young people.

• *Bible story wagon.* A Maryland church used a Bible story wagon that was a decorated car driven from neighborhood to neighborhood to present a Bible story one day each week. Stops were made in neighborhoods where VBS children lived.

- *Camp.* Make a special effort to get every VBS participant enrolled to go to camp.
- *Kid's Kamp.* This is a two-hour-per-night, one-night-per-week program combining activity with Bible teaching, much as the weekly club does.

Follow Up With Staff

Those committed workers who made VBS happen must not be overlooked in the follow-up phase. They deserve a big word of thanks for a job well done. This can be done with verbal thanks, an appreciation certificate or other recognition, a letter of thanks, recognition in the church paper, recognition in a worship service, or a dinner or coffee in their honor. Even though they did not choose to do the job with the goal to be thanked for it, their efforts should not go unrecognized.

Many VBS workers are teaching or assisting for the first time. Some of them would make excellent Sunday-school teachers or youth sponsors. Their names should be given to the responsible supervisors who can in turn enlist them for further training and/or service.

Follow Up With Evaluation

Evaluation of the program is an essential process if current strengths are to be retained and weaknesses are to be corrected. The following areas should be evaluated.

Director's Evaluation
The director should evaluate the total VBS process. What went well? What needs to be improved? Who worked well?

LINCOLN CHRISTIAN COLLEGE AND SEMINARY

Who needs help? A sample checklist appears below. One of the following evaluation notations should appear before each item: S—satisfactory, A—acceptable, U—unsatisfactory.

____ 1. Were teachers and helpers recruited early enough?

____ 2. Were supplies ordered soon enough for staff members to make adequate preparation for the school?

____ 3. Did teachers attend training sessions?

____ 4. Did the teachers have their activity books and samples of crafts prepared in advance?

____ 5. Did people in the community know about VBS in advance? Was publicity adequate?

____ 6. Was transportation available for those who needed it?

____ 7. Did we do a good job of recruiting unchurched children from the community?

____ 8. Did we make the best use of our space and equipment?

____ 9. Did we have adequate teachers and helpers?

____ 10. Did staff members understand their duties and fulfill them cheerfully and promptly?

____ 11. Did the pupils gain a new interest in missions?

____ 12. Was recreation properly planned and supervised for all ages?

____ 13. Was the worship program well planned? Did the pupils have a genuine worship experience?

____ 14. Was our closing program scheduled and advertised so that a majority of parents could attend?

____ 15. Was the closing program well organized?

____ 16. Were usable materials (visual packets, missionary packets, scissors, crayons, etc.) sorted and properly stored?

____ 17. Were adequate records kept? Will they be available to the director next year?

____ 18. Has provision been made for an evangelistic follow-up of new families contacted through VBS?

____ 19. Has worship and Sunday-school attendance increased as a result of VBS?

____ 20. Was the VBS material true to the Bible? Adequate?

Staff Evaluation

The VBS staff should be asked to fill out an evaluation form to be turned in to the director. A form such as the following would be helpful.

Department _____ Teacher ☐ Helper ☐ Supt. ☐
Name _____

I. Preparation
   1. How many department planning sessions did your superintendent conduct? ____ How many did you attend? ____
   2. Did these sessions help you in the following areas:
      a) Schedule ____ Yes ____ No
      b) Lesson preparation ____ Yes ____ No
      c) Crafts ____ Yes ____ No
      d) Other department activities ____ Yes ____ No
   3. Comments:

   4. Suggestions for next year:

II. Materials
   1. Printed Materials
      a) Were they suited to your age group? ____ Yes ____ No
      b) Were the visuals suitable? ____ Yes ____ No
      c) Were the suggested teaching methods helpful? ____ Yes ____ No
   2. Crafts
      a) Were they suitable to your age group? ____ Yes ____ No
      b) Were they correlated to course themes? ____ Yes ____ No
      c) Did you have adequate supplies? ____ Yes ____ No

3. Comments:

III. Classroom Organization
   1. Were you satisfied with the number of pupils in your class?____ Yes____ No How many did you have?____
   2. Did you receive the supplies and equipment you needed?____ Yes____ No
   3. Comments:

IV. Personnel
   1. What suggestions would help things run more smoothly for:
   Director:

   Superintendents:

   Missionary:

   Supply Chairman:

   Transportation Chairman:

   Teachers:

   Helpers:

   Kitchen Committee:

   Janitors:

   Worship Leader:

2. Who made an outstanding contribution to VBS?

V. Next Year
   1. What changes would you suggest for next year?

   2. Will you work again next year? ____ Yes ____ No
      ____ Same Capacity ____ Older Group ____ Younger
      Group

Teacher's Self-Evaluation

Teachers should be encouraged to evaluate themselves. Their self-evaluations are private domain, however, and should not be collected. A sample form follows. Each teacher could evaluate herself/himself on a scale of 1-5, with 5 being the highest.

____ 1. Did I learn all pupils' names?

____ 2. Did I prepare the materials well enough to present them well?

____ 3. Did I prepare spiritually through daily devotions and prayer?

____ 4. Did I hold the pupils' attention throughout the session?

____ 5. Did I relate the Scripture to pupils' daily lives?

____ 6. Did I relate the crafts to the lessons?

____ 7. Did I utilize my time in the classroom well?

____ 8. Did I maintain a Christian spirit throughout VBS?

____ 9. Have I planned ways to follow up my pupils after VBS is over?

Pupil Evaluation

Pupils' spiritual growth is a goal for VBS. Since that is true, their progress needs to be evaluated. This may be done by using the lesson aims, especially the specific observable behaviors, and developing a checklist for pupils at each age level. The teacher may fill out a checklist for each pupil. These may then be shared with parents when the teacher does a follow-up visit in the home.

Good evaluation provides rich information for future planning. A successful VBS is the result when one carefully plans, prayerfully prepares, energetically produces, and meticulously follows up.

Summary

Follow-up is as much a part of VBS as the theme song, crafts, or recruiting workers. Five areas of follow-up require attention: (1) materials and equipment, (2) records, (3) pupils, (4) staff, and (5) evaluation. And, in all things, remember to involve new families in your follow-up efforts. Vacation Bible School can be a program of outreach equalled by none other in your congregation's evangelistic efforts.

Project

Map out a practical, workable follow-up program for your VBS. Include dates and specific plans.

Bibliography

Freese, Doris A. *Vacation Bible School.* Wheaton, IL: Evangelical Teacher Training Association, 1977.

Getz, Gene. *The Vacation Bible School in the Local Church.* Chicago: Moody Press, 1962.

Chapter 9

EXTEND VBS MINISTRY
ALL SUMMER

As you read, think about the following:
1. What is a backyard VBS? How does it differ from a traditional VBS?
2. How can a mission VBS be used profitably?
3. What is a day camp? What is unique about it?
4. How can Bible clubs be used?
5. How can camping be tied into a total summer ministry?

VBS need not be confined to a week or two of the summer. A creative, ministry-oriented congregation could readily use the VBS concept of short-term ministry in several ways throughout the summer to extend its outreach and influence to an ever-enlarging group of people. The possibilities undoubtedly exceed those included in this chapter, but this does present some viable options for the congregation that is looking for a summer of ministry.

Backyard VBS

A backyard VBS is an especially useful tool in penetrating a community for the cause of Christ. Although a few churches have abandoned the traditional VBS at the church building in favor of backyard programs, this concept is probably best used as an evangelistic tool. More than a few congregations have conducted VBS as usual at the church building, making it primarily family oriented, then followed up with neighborhood backyard programs to extend their outreach and to make contact with new prospects for the church. Some new congregations who do not yet have permanent facilities, however, have used this concept to advantage.

Almost any congregation could find one or several homes whose residents (members of the congregation) will host a backyard VBS and serve as a contact/publicity person in their neighborhoods. The required space is a yard with water and toilet facilities readily available. Children may sit on the ground or around a picnic table. A garage would be helpful on rainy days.

Groups should be limited to ten to fifteen per yard. Sometimes only one age level could be placed in a yard if several homes in the same neighborhood were available.

Staffing for a backyard program is much simpler than for a large school at the church building. The most critical selection is the teacher—one for each four to eight children, depending upon the age level to be taught. A recreation leader would be helpful, but not absolutely essential. Perhaps the hostess could provide refreshments.

The backyard VBS should be planned for five days. The daily schedule needs to be amended to meet the special circumstances of an outside program. A sample schedule could be like the one that follows:

Recreation .... 10 minutes
Songs .... 5 minutes
Bible Lesson .... 30 minutes
    (Learning Activity, Story, Application)
Refreshments .... 10 minutes
Memory Verse .... 10 minutes
Songs .... 5 minutes
Crafts .... 15 minutes
Clean-up .... 5 minutes

Mission VBS

Some churches have planned a mission VBS to follow their regular VBS program. The teaching materials, already used once, can be utilized again to conduct a teaching program in a low income area, an orphanage, a summer resort, a city park (if permission can be secured), or the recreation room of an apartment complex (again, permission is essential). Some of the original VBS staff may be willing to serve another week in this kind of program. This is also an excellent project for high school or college youth.

Planning principles would be no different from those for a traditional VBS. Publicity must be carefully planned and implemented if the program is to achieve its purposes. Directors of this kind of VBS would do well to develop a schedule similar to that for a backyard VBS.

Some congregations have planned and conducted a mission VBS at a point far from home. High-school youth groups, for example, have developed and conducted VBS programs successfully on Indian reservations; in Mexico, Jamaica, Haiti, and Barbados; and for small mission churches, especially in Canada and on the East Coast of the United States. The possibilities are limitless, and the service is of lifelong value to the youth who participate.

Day Camp

Day camping is still another possibility for summer programming. A day camp is a teaching program conducted at a park, farm, or camp for a designated group of children (usually elementary school age). Day camps are sometimes conducted for five or more days in succession, but at other times they are designed for a day a week for five or more weeks preceding or following VBS. (The regular VBS curriculum may be adapted nicely for the sessions.)

The selection of a site for the day camp is of prime importance. It needs to be in a protected spot where some privacy is guaranteed. Water and rest rooms are essential; trails and swimming facilities are desirable. Furthermore, the site should be no more than thirty minutes from the church building.

Staffing must be done carefully. A director for the day camp functions much as a VBS director does. Counselors, one for each eight to ten children, carry the major load of Bible teaching. Craft leaders, a recreation leader, and a nature guide are other key personnel. Although children may bring sack lunches, a food chairman may be helpful for preparing drinks and snacks.

Pre-registration cannot be ignored for a day-camp program. The length of time spent in the program and the distance from the church building preclude the possibility of any guesswork in terms of numbers of participants.

Scheduling should take into account the fact that the program is conducted outdoors and for the entire day. A sample schedule can serve as a guide.

Meet at Church .... 9:00 a.m.
Arrive at Camp .... 9:30 a.m.
Bible Lesson .... 9:45 a.m.
    (Learning Activities, Story Application)
Team Activities I .... 10:55 a.m.
    (Crafts, Nature, or Recreation)
Lunch .... 11:50 a.m.
Team Activities II .... 12:40 p.m.
    (Crafts, Nature, or Recreation)
Team Activities III .... 1:35 p.m.
    (Crafts, Nature, or Recreation)
Missions .... 2:30 p.m.
Worship .... 3:05 p.m.
Depart Camp .... 3:30 p.m.
Arrive at Church .... 4:00 p.m.

A closing program is recommended to share learning with parents and other church members. It should follow the same guidelines as a VBS closing program.

Kid's Kamp and Bible Clubs

Some congregations have developed a Kid's Kamp or Bible Club program as a summer ministry to elementary children. It is conducted one day per week (either afternoon or evening) in the weeks following VBS. The program is usually two hours in length and follows a schedule similar to that in a two-hour VBS except with more emphasis on recreation and less on missions and/or crafts. Films are used at times in place of

crafts or Bible lessons. (The films would, of course, be Christian films.)

Planning parallels that done for VBS. Staffing needs are similar to those for VBS, as are publicity procedures. A closing program may also be desirable.

Camp

Church camp has proven to be a profound influence for many young people. An excellent VBS project is to set a goal to register *every* VBS student for camp.

Camps are usually the result of several churches cooperating together to develop a program of outdoor Christian education. Together they can offer better facilities, a wider variety of programming, and stronger staffing. Many camps have more than one week for each age level as well as camp programs for nearly every age level. It is not at all uncommon to find camps that conduct day camps for first and second graders, two-day programs for third and fourth graders, junior camps, junior high camps, senior camps, wilderness camps for the same variety of age levels, and even outpost camps that emphasize roughing it.

Some congregations conduct their own camps, all ages at one time, and make it a family affair. They rent a regular camp facility, but develop their own program, do their own staffing, and handle their own food service. This has been especially beneficial for churches a long distance from a regular church camp.

It is a wise extension of summer ministry to encourage not only churched, but also unchurched young people to attend one or more camp programs. It expands the VBS ministry many times over and solidifies a summer program when combined with other ideas presented in this chapter.

Summary

VBS alone is beneficial. VBS, combined with one or more of the summer ministries mentioned in this chapter, provides solid outreach, strong teaching, good fun, and increased fellowship, and results in new believers. Whether it is a backyard VBS, a mission VBS, a day camp, a Kid's Kamp or Bible club, or church camp, or any combination of these programs, the result can be an effective summer ministry.

Project

Choose one of the options suggested in this chapter and plan that program in detail for your congregation.

Bibliography

Mackey, Joy. *Raindrops Keep Falling on My Tent.* Wheaton: Victor Books, 1972.

Self, Margaret (ed.). *How to Plan and Organize Year-Round Bible Ministries.* Glendale, CA: Gospel Light, 1976.

Todd, Floyd and Pauline. *Camping for Christian Youth.* New York: Harper and Row Publishers, 1963.

Wright, Norman. *Help, I'm a Camp Counselor.* Glendale, CA: Gospel Light, 1968.

Chapter 10

TEACHING IN VBS

As you read, think about the following:
1. What are the most important characteristics for a teacher to understand about preschoolers?
2. What are the most important characteristics for a teacher to understand about an elementary-level child?
3. What are the most important characteristics for a teacher to understand about a youth?
4. What are the most important characteristics for a teacher to understand about adults?
5. What is total-session teaching? How can it be implemented in VBS?
6. What are the basic steps of lesson planning?
7. What are the suggested principles for classroom control?

The value of VBS is determined largely by what happens within the classrooms. Lives are changed or left untouched by the quality of Bible teaching in the classroom. Goals are achieved or left unattained on the basis of the teaching/learning interactions. The quality of teaching in VBS is so important that it deserves a section in a book devoted to VBS planning and preparation.

The teaching/learning process has at least four facets of supreme importance to the VBS teacher: (1) understanding the nature of the learner, (2) making every minute count, (3) planning an effective lesson, and (4) maintaining classroom control.

Understanding the Learner

No more than a thumbnail sketch of each age level can be made in the limited space of a small book. The teacher, however, should understand at least rudimentary details of human growth and development. This understanding is essential in building a suitable schedule (see Chapter 5) and choosing teaching methods.

Preschool

Preschoolers are growing, active, curious, thinking, feeling, independent people. And it is their activity, curiosity, ability to think, and independence that make them a joy to teach, yet pose a challenge to the inexperienced or insensitive teacher.

Preschoolers are growing physically. Although their height and weight do not increase dramatically from age two to six, there are vast physical changes, mostly those associated with motor development. The preschooler progresses from scribble art to definite shapes and forms in his drawing efforts. He learns to jump, run, and manipulate objects with his hands. Because of so much muscle development, he is active. He explores by touching, smelling, or tasting objects.

The preschooler is a word sponge. His intellectual development is rapid under normal circumstances, and a large portion of that intelligence increase is attributable to language development. Yet, his language is concrete; his understanding is literal. Therefore, the teacher must carefully choose the words by which he communicates the Christian faith.

The preschooler cannot reason, analyze, or synthesize information like an adult can. He is not yet ready for logical thinking. He is easily confused by what he sees. For example, he cannot visualize two masses of clay or water with unequal dimensions as possessing the same weight, even if he watched someone manipulate the clay or water from one shape to another. His attention fixes on one detail—height or length or width, for example—and he judges all masses by that detail.

An effective preschool teacher is clearly aware of the child's language and logical thinking limitations. He does not depreciate the worth of the child because of his inability to think as an adult. Rather he chooses concrete words, centers the lesson on one theme, uses concrete experiences such as life-related learning centers, and chooses an abundance of visual aids to convey Bible truth.

Preschoolers are imitators. Their play illustrates that very well. When a preschooler plays, he imitates life. He loves to pretend, and he uses "real life" ideas, information, and behavior to provide content for his play activity. This is why guided play can be such a productive learning tool in Christian education: the teacher directs the child's attention to particular "real life" settings and then uses Bible words and thoughts in the midst of the child's re-enactment of life.

Active—imitative—verbal—concrete, literal thinker—all are descriptions of a preschooler. All form the basis for the way a preschool child learns. The imaginative teacher will be aware of it and capitalize upon it.

Educable Mentally Retarded Children

If you have a preschool EMR child in your VBS, you may notice little difference in him and the other preschoolers. Generally, most preschool activities are sensory oriented and will assist in the development of the EMR child. He will need personal attention and much repetition.

The older EMR child will want to be with his peers, but he will learn more slowly than they do. He will have trouble with abstract ideas and generalizations, and his reading and writing skills will be limited. His two most frequent behavior problems will be withdrawal and rebellion. He is capable of understanding spiritual truths, including the concept of salvation.

Visit the EMR student in his home. Also gain information from trained workers to whom his parents refer you. Love and accept him as he is and set reasonable specific goals for him. (For further information, see resources in back of book.)

Children: Grades 1-6

Some major changes occur during the elementary-school years. This is quite evident when comparing a first grader with a sixth grader. While some changes are physical, the major growth occurs in the intellectual and psychological facets of personality.

These are sometimes called the latent years of physical growth. The child grows, but usually in a steady, nondramatic way. Motor development approaches adult standards by the end of the twelfth year. Elementary-age children are active, apt to overdo, and curiously move from one activity to another if they are not adequately challenged intellectually.

Without a doubt, the major physical change in any young person's life is the onset of puberty, an event that does happen to some fifth- and sixth-grade girls. Before the onset of puberty, these girls experience a growth spurt that leaves them towering above most boys the same age.

Learning to read is probably the biggest intellectual achievement of the elementary years. Now language can be used for both oral and visual communication, a significant achievement in a young life. Yet the differences in rate of achievement in reading differentiate among children and carry powerful connotations of personal worth for the child, depending upon how "good" or "bad" he perceives himself to be in comparison with others.

Most elementary children are curious, if they are encouraged and permitted to be. Interests develop during this time, although they may shift from one area to another prior to fifth or sixth grade.

Girls generally excel in verbal fluency and reading while boys are superior in mathematical reasoning and spatial manipulation. Consequently, boys and girls approach learning differently, and they respond differently to various teaching methods.

The first grader, and most second graders, think much as preschoolers do: pre-logically, literally, and based upon sensory experience. But sometime near the age of eight, a child begins to manipulate sizes and shapes in his head. He learns that a factor can be constant, even though external characteristics change. This progression makes it possible for him to understand cause-and-effect relationships, to draw hypotheses, and to do mathematical and scientific reasoning.

The elementary child becomes increasingly independent from family and begins to rely on friends and peers for ego strength. But as independent as the elementary child may seem, he still needs the affirmation of parents and teachers, provided by firm, consistent discipline and loving acceptance of him as a person.

Elementary children begin to see moral decisions in a context. Younger elementary children will still be rules oriented, but older children can assume another person's point of view, allowing them to consider possible options for action. It is also during this time that they come to a rudimentary understanding of salvation and their need for it if they are exposed to Bible teaching.

The wise elementary teacher plans with these characteristics in mind. He designs productive activity into the lesson. He plans for some opportunities for independent learning. He is not content to accept simple "parroting" of Bible information as an indicator of genuine understanding. Yet he teaches to bring the child to know Jesus Christ, realizing that to know Christ is to embark on a lengthy maturation process.

Youth

Youth, those people from twelve to eighteen years of age, are complex creatures, no longer little children, but most assuredly not yet adults. Youth is a period of intense feelings, significant growth, and life-shaping decisions.

The teen years are marked by all of the dramatic physical changes that spell the difference between childhood and adulthood. The majority of youth will experience puberty during the junior-high years. (Some girls may reach it during the fifth- or sixth-grade year, as indicated earlier. Some boys may reach early high school before they experience this physical process.)

The vast majority of the concerns of teenagers centers around the physical. Their sense of self-worth is affected by physical characteristics and appearance. Intense, sometimes frightening, sexual feelings awaken. Teens live, breathe, and eat their relationships, especially those with the opposite sex. Dating is an all-consuming interest for most teenagers.

Teens are "here and now" people, even though they are capable of long-range planning. Their behavior is much more apt to be dictated by feelings than by reasoned consideration of the future.

Peer pressure is constant and sometimes extraordinarily painful for youth. Yet it is an essential intermediate step in making the shift from being a totally dependent child to an interdependent adult. Some teens are too dependent upon peer support, to be sure, and cliques can result in negative pressure. But even so, the process is important. The key is to recognize the importance of peer pressure and to help the youth learn how to handle it.

Teens are also idealistic. They easily determine how things "ought to be," then find it difficult to reconcile injustice, imperfection, suffering, and disappointment with that ideal. It is this, as much as anything else, that causes the emergence of doubts. It is not uncommon for youth to express spiritual doubts and to ask penetrating, difficult questions. It may, in fact, be an important step in the process of exchanging a childish faith for one that can mature and become productive.

A teacher of teens cannot ignore the needs and interests of those in his class. No longer can he teach them as children; they must be treated as young adults, still dependent, but at the same time young adults who can think, reason, and question their faith and its application.

Adults

Adults are those people over eighteen and/or out of high school. They comprise over half of nearly any congregation. They are "adults" for nearly three-fourths of the life span. There are distinct differences between young adults, middle adults, and older adults, all of which must be taken into account by the teacher. But as interesting as those differences are, space does not permit development of them.

There are some distinctives of adult learners of every age, however, and these must be taken into consideration when teaching adults. The first distinctive is that an adult is a unique learner. One cannot make a generalized statement about an adult learner in the same sense one can about younger ages. There is no physical uniformity, no likeness of thinking style, no uniform procedure in making emotional adjustments. He is unique.

The adult learns as a total person. The way he is dealing with internal changes affects his perceptions and reactions in learning situations.

The adult learner brings valuable experience with him to learning situations. This allows him to lend significant insights to it. These must not be ignored.

An adult learns best when he is an active participant in the learning situation. He learns by interacting with others, by identification with a group, by not only hearing information, but also figuring out how to use it.

An adult has learned only when he has assimilated information into personal behavior. Simply acquiring Bible information as a factual exercise is inadequate: the material must alter attitudes and behavior.

Although an adult teacher certainly must become conversant with the special needs of his adults, he must also take into account the foregoing principles if he is to teach successfully. It is never enough merely to present facts—he must always seek response as well.

Making Every Minute Count

Every minute in VBS should contribute to the overall learning goals for the program. It is a sin to waste precious minutes because of failure to plan every VBS activity to contribute to the teaching for the day. Some call this *total-session teaching*. Whatever it is called, correlation of every activity and careful selection of every teaching tool is the goal.

Chapter 5 introduced the idea of tying together every segment of VBS into a unified whole. The sample schedules included in the chapter reflect that same concern. Whether one is involved in worship, missions, learning centers, Bible study, recreation, or crafts, a common thread must tie the experiences together. That thread is the learning goal for the session. Each part develops, reinforces, or applies the goal. Note the following sketch:

Learning Centers

Many publishers now suggest the use of learning centers as a part of lesson development. Those centers are usually used to provide an introduction to the Bible concepts for the day, in much the same way that the traditional "pre-session" time was used. The shift from "pre-session" to "learning centers" helps to identify the activities as part of the lesson development.

A learning center is an area where pupils may actively pursue a learning activity designed to introduce them to Bible facts, concepts, or understandings. It is desirable that students be given a choice of activities, each center featuring a different type of activity with differing degrees of difficulty (especially for elementary-age children). Preschool learning centers must always be manned by a teacher who can direct thinking and conversation to the Bible truth for the day. That is not absolutely necessary for elementary children who can listen to or read instructions for completing an activity.

Learning centers can include a wide variety of activities, limited only by the teacher's imagination. The only requirement is that the activity carry out the lesson theme. This thumbnail sketch of several possibilities, along with appropriate age levels, will stimulate the teacher's imagination:

God's Wonders: shells, stones, leaves, flowers, animals, magnets, prisms, etc.—preschoolers

Blocks: building blocks, toys with wheels—preschoolers

Puzzles: large wooden inlay puzzles—preschoolers

Books: children's books—preschoolers and elementary children

Housekeeping: dolls, dishes, stove, etc.—preschoolers

Music: records and cassette tapes for preschoolers and elementary children to listen to; writing new words to existing tunes and/or making song comparisons—elementary children

Art: finger painting and easel painting—preschoolers; cartoon strips, maps, mobiles, murals, montages, slide presentations (with write-on slides), and collages—elementary children

Drama: pantomime the Bible story, skits, role play to apply Bible truth, puppet shows, play reading, and acting out Bible-time interviews—elementary children

Written Activities: letter writing, diary, news story, open-ended story to apply Bible truth, writing poetry, writing a prayer, verse scramble, word puzzle, questions to answer from a Bible text—elementary children and youth

Games: Bible-verse games, facts games, review games, application games—elementary children and youth

Many of these same activities used for learning centers are effective teaching methods when used at other points in the lesson presentation. Some activities designated for elementary children could also be used as methods for youth and adults, either in the fellowship or Bible-study times. Make sure these activities are appropriate to the age level of the group.

Most curriculum materials suggest possible learning centers for preschool and elementary classrooms. These should be helpful to the teacher. At times, however, he may need to alter the suggestions and develop his own learning centers.

Bible Exploration and Application

Bible exploration and application is simply transferring a continuation of what began in the learning centers for preschoolers and elementary children to the larger group. It is akin to what has usually been called "the lesson," i.e., the formal examination of Biblical material and how it applies to life. For preschoolers, it is a time of identifying the Bible thought used in the learning centers with its source, the Bible. For elementary children, it is using the learning-center activities to present the Bible facts and applications. For youth and adults, it requires careful selection of activities to get them into the Bible for themselves, allowing some time for personal and/or small-group study followed by reporting and discussion in the larger group.

The primary method for teaching preschoolers is storytelling followed by a pupil's book or make-it activity. This kind of telling is particularly effective when it builds upon the children's involvement in carefully planned learning centers.

Storytelling is sometimes used for elementary children as well as for preschoolers. But a wider variety of methods is available to the creative teacher. Most of the time the children will have completed learning-center activities that present the Bible information. They can report these during the Bible-study time, leaving the teacher to fill in missed facts or inadequate information. Then the application can be developed using discussion, art, music, drama, case studies, or any of the other activities suggested for learning centers. (Of course, application activities should differ from what was done in the learning centers for any given lesson.)

A wide range of activities is available to stimulate youth and adults. These, too, are chosen on the basis of what will best carry out the goal of the lesson. Seven categories encompass the options. These, with some possible variations, are listed for the benefit of the teacher/aid:

Lecture: films, monologues, listening teams, symposium, panel discussions, reports

Discussion: agree/disagree statements, brainstorming, buzz groups, case studies, debates, problem solving, completion statements, neighbor nudge, picture responses, word association

Writing: letter writing, diary or journal, memo writing, news story, poetry, prayer writing, self-evaluation, word puzzles, acrostics, headline writing, scrambled verses

Drama: pantomimes, role plays, skits, simulated TV programs

Art: banners, bumper stickers, campaign badges, collages, montages, graffiti posters, murals, maps, rebuses, graphs, mobiles, charts, puppets, slide making

Music: concept and song match, hymn paraphrase, musical commercial, writing new words for a familiar tune, hymn and Scripture comparison

Research: field trips, book reports, question research, topical reports

The choice of what activities to use for any age level depends upon six factors: (1) aim of the lesson, (2) size of the group, (3) size of the room, (4) resources and supplies available, (5) abilities and interests of the students, and (6) time available. The first factor in particular must never be ignored.

Worship

Worship is response to God and the truth of His Word. It should be planned with such lofty ideals in mind. The point for this particular section is to emphasize the need to correlate the worship activities with the lesson theme for the day. Songs, Scriptures, devotional thoughts, whatever activities are included in the worship session, must contribute to the development of lesson aims.

Recreation and Refreshments

Even recreation and refreshments can be used to contribute to the lesson aim. Some teachers' books suggest games and snacks to tie in with the lesson theme. But even if the curriculum provides little or no help at this point, the teacher can rename old familiar games or adapt games to fit the lesson themes. Refreshments can often be correlated with the lesson, too, especially for younger children.

Expressional Activities

Crafts and other expressional activities should also present and reinforce the Bible truth for the day. No activity should be included that fails to meet this test, regardless of its creativity and durability. (A possible exception would be activities that contribute to some overall VBS goal, such as intergenerational activities. But even then, every effort should be bent toward correlating the activity with the lesson theme.)

As Chapter 5 pointed out, the expressional time need not be confined to the traditional craft idea. Choirs, drama groups, puppet groups, film-making groups, and service projects may be valuable as teaching tools for older groups.

It is imperative to make every VBS minute count. That can be done best when every segment of the VBS session is viewed as a means of developing the lesson theme.

Planning an Effective Lesson

Having a variety of learning centers and teaching methods at one's disposal is one thing, but another is to use that information, plus the curriculum materials at hand, to develop a creative, appealing Bible lesson. But it is a task that can be done rather simply if some basic principles are followed.

Getting Ready for the Bible Lesson

The first step in lesson preparation is to spend time studying the Bible text for personal edification. Too often lesson preparation begins with the teacher's book instead of with God's Word. All of the principles for effective personal Bible study should be followed at this juncture. The focus of attention should be the Word and how it applies to the teacher's life. After the teacher has spent adequate time in study of the Word, he is ready to think about how to teach that Bible truth.

Next, the teacher should determine the central truth, or the focus, for the Bible lesson. This will be the thread that ties everything together for the teaching session. This focus is determined by three factors: (1) the message of the Biblical text, (2) the age level of the learners, and (3) the specific needs of the learners. Of course, the focus must be Biblically sound, but it must also be life-related, if it is to be meaningful to the learner. (If the VBS curriculum you have chosen contains a theme chart, you will note that there is a suggested focus for each lesson.) The focus should be stated in one simple sentence in order to make sure it is clearly understood. That statement will help to decide what material to include in the lesson and what to omit.

The third step is to concentrate on the lesson aims. At this point, the curriculum materials may be helpful. Usually, there are rather specific statements of intended learning outcomes written in the lesson materials. These should not be accepted without evaluation, however, for they may need alteration or revision to meet the central focus chosen for the lesson or to meet specific needs and capabilities of the class for which the lesson is intended. These outcomes should be stated in specific, overtly observable, measurable behaviors that will result from interaction from this Bible passage.

Building the Bible Lesson

The teacher is then ready to build the Bible lesson. Each Bible lesson has four distinct parts (at least this is true beyond the preschool ages, although all elements are still present in the preschool as well). The first part is the attention step, usually achieved with learning centers for preschoolers and elementary children. The teacher should consult the teacher's materials to find the suggestions made by the curriculum writer. All of them may be quite acceptable for the focus and aims stated for the lesson, in which case they can be used. Sometimes all of them are not acceptable, however, because of changes in focus or aims or because of capabilities or needs of the specific class, in which case the teacher should make the necessary changes.

The second part of the Bible lesson is the Bible exploration phase. Again, the teacher should consult the teacher's materials for suggestions made by the curriculum writer and make any necessary changes according to the focus of the lesson and the needs of the student. Keep in mind also that many VBS publishers include more material than the teacher will need, due to the variance in time schedules for schools. Choose those ideas that will best meet the needs of your students. Substitute new ideas developed from the suggestions in this chapter.

Application forms the third phase of the Bible lesson. It is necessary for the teacher to help the pupil find out what responses are appropriate for the Bible materials. The same procedure is followed in planning this section of the lesson. Use whatever is appropriate from the materials; eliminate what is not, and add new ideas.

The final part is decision. At this point, the teacher leads the pupils to make a commitment to the specific response they will make to the Bible material. The preparation procedure is exactly the same as for other sections of the lesson.

A teacher who follows this lesson preparation procedure will have little difficulty in creating a Bible lesson that is uniquely his. There is absolutely no reason for a lesson to appear canned nor for it to be dull and boring if the teacher prepares well. Curriculum materials are designed to be tools rather than taskmasters.

Maintaining Classroom Control

Perhaps the most severe problem to confront a teacher in VBS is maintaining classroom control. Although this is always a challenge to any teacher in any classroom situation, it is sometimes more intense in VBS because of longer sessions that meet every day. Sometimes familiarity breeds contempt. Therefore, it is helpful for the VBS teacher to have a grasp on the basics in discipline.

Causes of Misbehavior

Misbehavior stems from a variety of causes. In fact, two students who misbehave in the same way may be doing it for totally different reasons. It is helpful to have a checklist of causes in mind in order to prevent those that are under the control of the teacher.

Sometimes misbehavior is due to physical discomfort. Inadequate lighting, poor ventilation, rooms that are too hot or too cold, sun glare, and furniture inappropriate to the age result in restlessness, yawning, inattention, giggling, fidgeting, and whispering. Not all of these causes may be under the teacher's control, but many are.

Other discipline problems occur because of poor teaching practices. When there is nothing planned for the student to do when he arrives in the classroom, he will find something to do (and not what his teacher would have chosen). When there are inadequate activities and/or mental challenges for the pupil, he is bored. When the teacher has to interrupt a presentation to find needed materials, the pupil's attention wanders. When inappropriate methods are used, the pupil becomes bored. In short, the teacher himself controls much of the behavior that occurs in his classroom.

Some misbehavior problems are due to surplus energy. Writing notes, throwing paper wads, teasing, and other forms of horseplay are often the symptoms, but the root cause is a teaching style that ignores the learner's need for involvement. The teacher can correct that by using learning centers and other stimulating methods to involve the pupil in the learning process.

Discipline problems sometimes occur because of an uncomplicated desire to be noticed. Examples of typical attention-getting behavior are practical jokes, teasing, showing off, bragging, arguing, and impudence.

Other misbehavior is caused by subtle, internal forces. Undesirable aggressive behaviors such as bullying and argumentativeness are often the result of home situations or parental disciplinary patterns. So are lying, refusal to obey, destructiveness, profanity, cruelty to others, and withdrawal from the situation.

Simply identifying the cause of misbehavior is not enough, of course. But it does make understanding and dealing with the misbehavior more specific, practical, and attainable.

Correcting Misbehavior

The ideal classroom management principle is to prevent all misbehavior. That is impossible, however, for reasons cited above. So try as he will, there is no teacher who can prevent *every* misbehavior problem. As long as a classroom contains "real live kids," a teacher will have to contend with "real live discipline problems." He may as well accept that fact.

Discipline is sometimes approached in a vindictive manner. The teacher seems to be getting even with the student. Other teachers correct as if discipline were retribution, i.e., if a pupil has done evil, he must suffer the consequences. Some teachers discipline with fear tactics. But none of these three is adequate for a Christian teacher whose goal is to bring the student to a point of responsibility and Christlikeness. Such a goal colors attitude and action in the disciplinary process.

A few simple principles provide guidance for the teacher who must correct misbehavior. These are very important!

1. Always respect the personality of the child. A disciplinary action is no call for ridicule, depreciation of personality, nor any other form of put-down. Remember that the offender is still a human being.
2. Punishment may be necessary. Children do not always respond to reasoning.
3. The desired result of disciplinary action is changed behavior. Punishment, alone, is not adequate. That punishment must result in positive action.
4. Be firm, fair, and consistent in classroom expectation and corrections.

When misbehavior occurs in the classroom, a teacher needs a ready plan of action. The following plan has been shown to be beneficial to teachers everywhere:

1. Decide whether to deal with the misbehavior or to ignore it. This requires some definition of the boundaries for behavior before entering the classroom. Very seldom can misbehavior be ignored successfully, but if it is attention getting in nature, it may be better to ignore the behavior than to give it the desired attention. The determining factor is whether the behavior is disruptive to others.
2. If the behavior requires response, the focus should be on the behavior itself, not on the worth of the person involved. Guilt must be established beyond the shadow of a doubt. The child must know that he is acceptable as a person, even when his behavior is totally inappropriate. It is helpful for the teacher to state what he saw, then let the child agree or disagree.
3. Choose the punishment. If at all possible, the punishment should be a natural outcome of the misbehavior, e.g., removing the child from misused materials or sitting quietly

apart from the group as a result of excessive noise. The degree of punishment should be commensurate with the misdemeanor and appropriate for the age level and individual. Punishment should not humiliate or cause suffering.
4. Let the child know why he is being punished. Restate the rules. It is also helpful to have the child state his understanding of why he is receiving punishment. Make this a time of teaching.
5. After the child has been punished, reassure him of his personal worth. Be sympathetic, yet firm and businesslike.

A teacher who loves children, who plans his teaching carefully, and who handles the classroom firmly and consistently will have relatively few serious behavior challenges. The reminder can be handled in a constructive, instructive way so that children may continue to develop toward the goal of self-discipline.

Summary

Teaching in VBS is a challenge. But it is a rewarding challenge if the teacher understands his job. An effective teacher first understands the age level he is teaching. Rather than expressing frustration with activity and curiosity, he will channel those very natural characteristics into productive learning. Then he will plan every minute of the VBS session so that each activity contributes to the development of the lesson aim. He will carefully prepare his lesson to get attention, explore the Bible, examine possible applications, and make a decision about use of the material. Finally he will utilize the principles of effective classroom management to assure a productive, peaceful, goal-directed classroom.

Projects
1. Plan a lesson for VBS using the principles outlined in this chapter.
2. Interview two or three effective veteran teachers about how they handle classroom discipline.

Bibliography
Daniel, Eleanor; Gresham, Charles; and Wade, John. *Introduction to Christian Education.* Cincinnati: Standard Publishing, 1980.
Leavitt, Guy P. *Teach With Success,* revised by Eleanor Daniel. Cincinnati: Standard Publishing, 1978.
Richards, Lawrence O. *Creative Bible Teaching.* Chicago: Moody Press, 1970.

Chapter 11

A GUIDE FOR
TEACHING THIS BOOK

Session 1: VBS—Past, Present, and Future

Goal: The pupil will be able to identify the major developments in the history of VBS.

Xcite
As the class members arrive, ask them to complete this sentence: "My first memory of VBS is . . ." Give them three or four minutes to complete this. Then ask them to form groups of three to discuss their responses for another three or four minutes. Then lead a brief general discussion.

Xplore
1. Present the introductory material in Chapter 1.
2. Have the students brainstorm for five minutes to suggest values of VBS. Tell the class that ideas—no comments—are to be stated during the five minutes. Then take another five minutes to evaluate the responses.
3. Present the historical material about VBS from Chapter 1.

Xpand   VBS Trivia
1. Have someone prepared to make a brief report on the history of VBS in your congregation.
2. Discuss: How can we be sure that VBS has a solid future in this congregation? Reach specific decisions.
3. Conclude with a challenge to make VBS a ministry.

Assignment
1. Read Chapters 1 and 2 before next session.
2. Complete the project at the end of Chapter 1.

Session 2: Develop a Plan of Action

Goal: The pupil will be able to apply the initial steps of VBS preparation to a specific situation.

Xcite

As the class members arrive, ask them to think of the best VBS they ever participated in and why it was so. Have them form groups of four to discuss this. After five minutes, lead a general discussion centered around that theme. Answers may be numerous, but all of them are probably indicative of the fact that the program was carefully planned and executed.

Xplore
1. Display a chart showing the four initial steps to be done in planning a VBS.
2. Have four people prepared to make brief reports (four to six minutes) on each of the four steps of preparation.

Xpand

Divide the class into groups of four. Give each the following data:

> You will be VBS director for a small church. Last year there were thirty-five children (ages two through grade eight) in VBS. Your community has a population of 5,000. Most of the churches in town do not have VBS. Those who do conduct VBS have it for one week during the morning, early in June. You are to use this data to do the preliminary planning for your VBS. You may use your book to help, if you need to.

Allot twenty-five to thirty minutes for this, followed by reports. Make any necessary comments or corrections.

Assignment
Read Chapter 3 before next session.

Session 3: Select Curriculum Materials

Goal: The pupil will be able to select curriculum materials on the basis of objective criteria.

Xcite
Ask the students to work in pairs to discuss: "If I were the

writer of curriculum materials for VBS, I would . . ." Allot five to seven minutes for this. Follow it with a general discussion.

Xplore
Present the criteria mentioned in this chapter, illustrating them with sample materials.

Xpand
Divide the class into department groups. Give each group that part of the curriculum for the VBS. Ask the groups to evaluate the materials using the criteria in this chapter. Allot twenty-five to thirty minutes for this, followed by a reporting session.

Assignment
Read Chapter 4 for next session.

Session 4: Recruit and Train Workers

Goal: The pupil will be able to apply recruitment and training principles to a specific VBS situation.

Xcite
Give each person the acrostic below and ask him to complete it by using qualities of an effective teacher. Sample responses are included.

T-eachable
E-nthusiastic
A-vailable
C-onverted
H-onest
E-ager
R-eputable

Allot four or five minutes. Then have a reporting session.

Xplore
1. Display a chart showing the four steps for recruiting and training workers.
2. Briefly summarize each step.

Xpand
Present the same case study as was used in Session 2. If possible, form the same groups. Ask them to determine

needed staff, write a sample job description for a teacher, and plan training for their VBS. Allot twenty-five to thirty minutes for this. Follow with reports.

Assignment
Read Chapter 5 before next session.

Session 5: Plan a Workable Time Schedule

Goal: The pupil will be able to plan a time schedule for his church situation and age level, using accepted guidelines.

Xcite
As the students arrive, ask them to work together in groups of two and write up what they consider to be a typical VBS schedule, on the basis of their experience. Allot four or five minutes for this. Then let them report by placing their schedules on the chalkboard or newsprint. Compare the responses, noting similarities and differences.

Xplore
1. Point out the four guidelines that should be taken into consideration when building a schedule.
2. Have the original groups of two list all of the activities that must be included in a time schedule. Allot four or five minutes for this. Then have the groups report. Add details to each as they are mentioned.

Xpand
Divide the class members into groups by the age group of their choice. Then have each age level plan a schedule for VBS for this congregation, taking into account the principles in this chapter. Allot twenty minutes for this. Follow with reports. Critique the results.

Assignment
1. Read Chapter 6 for next week.
2. Prepare at least one publicity piece to be used for VBS.

Session 6: Publicize!

Goal: The pupil will be able to plan a workable publicity program for the VBS in his congregation.

Xcite

As the pupils arrive, have them display their publicity items for VBS. When most people have arrived, have each person tell why he chose the publicity item he did and to whom it would appeal.

Xplore

1. Present the four publicity principles in this chapter, using sample items to show how the principles apply.
2. Lead a five-minute brainstorming session to list as many publicity items as possible. Evaluate the responses.

Xpand

Divide the class into groups of five. Ask each group to design a publicity program for your VBS. Allot twenty-five minutes for this. Have the groups report. Evaluate the reports.

Assignment

Read Chapter 7 for the next session.

Session 7: Build a Closing Program

Goal: The pupil will be able to plan an effective closing program for his VBS.

Xcite

Ask the class members to complete the following sentence as they enter the classroom: "When I think of closing programs, I . . ." Allot three or four minutes for this. Then share the responses in a brief discussion.

Xplore

Have two people prepared to present the material in "Closing Activities" and "Closing Demonstration Program."

Xpand

Divide the class by age-level interests. Give them the curriculum materials for their age level. Ask them to examine the materials for suggested closing program ideas. Then have them plan a closing program. Allot twenty-five minutes for this. Allow each group to report.

Assignment

Read Chapters 8 and 9 for next session.

Session 8: Follow Up!

Goal: The pupil will be able to plan a feasible VBS follow-up program for his congregation.

Xcite
Ask the pupils to decide whether they agree or disagree with the following statements:
1. VBS is over when the closing program is completed.
2. It is possible to make VBS last all year long.
3. VBS isn't VBS unless it is held at the church building.
4. When excess materials are put away, the VBS director's job is done.

Give the pupils three or four minutes to answer these. Then lead a general discussion about each item.

Xplore
Have five people present reports on VBS follow-up—one for each section in Chapter 8 and one for the whole of Chapter 9. Limit each report to five minutes.

Xpand
Divide the class into groups of three. Have the groups plan a feasible follow-up program for your VBS.

Assignment
Read Chapter 10 before next session.

Session 9: Teaching in VBS (I)

Goal: The pupil will be able to plan an effective Bible lesson for a specific class.

Xcite
As the class members arrive, ask them to choose one of four groups (preschool, elementary, youth, adult) according to their particular interests. Each group is to develop a chart listing the major characteristics of that age level and also include suggestions for how to incorporate these into their teaching. Allot fifteen minutes for this. Have each group present a report of its work. Add any appropriate comments and information.

Xplore
Prepare one VBS lesson from the current curriculum series.

Teach it, asking class members to act like pupils of the age level for which it is intended. After it is finished, go over each part of it, asking pupils what happened and why it may have been done that way. Emphasize total-session teaching.

Xpand
Have the pupils briefly look at one more lesson from the curriculum to see how total-session teaching is utilized. Have them suggest better ways the lesson idea could be developed.

Assignment
Complete project 2 from Chapter 10 before next session.

Session 10: Teaching in VBS (II)

Goal: The pupil will be able to plan an effective Bible lesson for a specific class.

Xcite and Xplore
As the pupils arrive, have them again elect an age level of their choice. Give each group a copy of the VBS curriculum materials for that age level. Ask them to plan a Bible lesson designed for the age level, following the procedure suggested in this chapter. (Assign which lesson to use so that all groups are doing the same one.) Ask them to record the lesson plan on a sheet of newsprint. Allot thirty to forty minutes for this. Then have each group report.

Xpand
Ask each person to report on his assignment for this week. Review the principles for effective classroom management.

To close, ask each person to answer: "I have decided that when I teach in VBS, I will . . ."

RESOURCES

Bible Learning Activities

Burrage, Barbara, *Bible Quizzerama*, Standard Publishing.
Dilley, Romilda, *Bible Crostics*, Standard Publishing.
Easy Bible Quizzes for All Ages, Standard Publishing.
Faust, David and Candy, *Puppet Plays With a Point*, Standard
    Publishing.
Gay, Marcina, *Bible Quizzes for Kids*, Standard Publishing.
Hein, Lucille, *Enjoying the Outdoors With Children*, Associa-
    tion Press.
Hodson, Violet, *Puppet Plays*, Standard Publishing.
Parables of Jesus (classroom puzzle book—8 each of 6 differ-
    ent puzzles), Standard Publishing.
Priddy, Linda, *Writing Fun for Kids: Living for Jesus*, Standard
    Publishing.
———, *Writing Fun for Kids: The Bible and Me*, Standard Pub-
    lishing.
Puzzles From Acts (classroom puzzle book—8 each of 6 dif-
    ferent puzzles), Standard Publishing.
Rodrick, Bruce, *Teaching With Puppets*, Standard Publishing.
Shelly and Grossman, *Ecology*, Grosset and Dunlap.
Sherlock, Connie, *Life of Jesus Think 'N Check Quizzes*,
    Standard Publishing.
Skinner, Donna, *File Folder Learning Centers*, Standard Pub-
    lishing.
———, *75 + 1 = Fun* (learning games for children), Standard
    Publishing.
202 Things to Do, Gospel Light Publications.

Children's Bible Study Aids

Basic Bible Dictionary, Standard Publishing.
Tester, Sylvia Root, *The World Into Which Jesus Came*, Stan-
    dard Publishing.

Crafts

(Consult the following resources to supplement packaged crafts supplied by the publishing house that produces your VBS course.)

Biddle, Maureen, *50 Craft Projects With Bible Verses and Patterns*, Standard Publishing.

Bible Patterns and Stencils, Standard Publishing.

Bible Stencils, Standard Publishing.

Craft Digest, Follett Books.

Creative Craft Ideas for All Ages, Standard Publishing.

Dahl, Anna M., *Handwork Patterns for the Whole Year*, Standard Publishing.

Dorfé, *86 Crafts From Plastic Castoffs*, Standard Publishing.

52 Preschool Activity Patterns, Standard Publishing.

Frost, Marie, *52 Primary Crafts*, Standard Publishing.

——, *52 Nursery Patterns*, Standard Publishing.

Graff, Michelle, and Reese, Loretta, *34 Craft Stick Projects*, Standard Publishing.

Gramelsbach, Helen W., *71 Creative Bible Story Projects*, Standard Publishing.

——, *30 Bible Story Projects to Make*, Standard Publishing.

Hammond, Phyllis E., *What to Do—and Why*, Judson Press.

Handcraft Encyclopedia, Gospel Light Publications.

Hart, Joanna, *52 Preschool Crafts*, Standard Publishing.

Karch, Pat, *51 Paper Craft Projects*, Standard Publishing.

Kinser, Charleen, *Outdoor Art for Kids*, Follett Books.

Lennander, Jean, *58 Wallpaper Crafts*, Standard Publishing.

Now What Can We Do? Gospel Light Publications.

Outdoor Living Skills Instructor's Manual, American Camping Association.

Pattern Encyclopedia, Gospel Light Publications.

Plan and Do Projects, David C. Cook Publishing Company.

Projects and Patterns for Nursery Leaders, David C. Cook Publishing Company.

Projects and Patterns for Kindergarten Leaders, David C. Cook Publishing Company.

Quick Crafts for Sunday School Teachers, David C. Cook Publishing Company.

Reese, Loretta, *50 Craft Ideas With Patterns*, Standard Publishing.

54 Crafts With Easy Patterns, Standard Publishing.
Rowen, Delores, *Easy-to-Make Crafts: Children 3-11 Years,* Gospel Light Publications.
Rowland, Jacqueline, *52 Middler/Junior Crafts,* Standard Publishing.
Russell, Susan, *52 Teen Crafts,* Standard Publishing.
Self, Margaret, *158 Things to Make,* Gospel Light Publications.
301 Creative Crafts for All Occasions, Standard Publishing.
Vonk, Idalee, *52 Elementary Patterns,* Standard Publishing.
Year 'Round Preschool Activity Patterns, Standard Publishing.

Music

(Consult the following resources to supplement the correlated VBS songbook supplied by the publishing house that produces your VBS course.)

Celebrate, Pennsylvania Council of Churches.
Frost, Marie, *Songs for Preschoolers,* Standard Publishing.
Little Ones Sing (Early Childhood), Gospel Light Publications.
Preschoolers Sing, David C. Cook Publishing Company.
Primaries and Juniors Sing, David C. Cook Publishing Company.
Sing, Look, Do, Standard Publishing.
Sing Praises (Children), Gospel Light Publications.
Songs for Preschool Children, Standard Publishing.
Sunday School Sings, Gospel Light Publications.
Youth Sings, Gospel Light Publications.

Teaching Mentally Retarded Students

Perske, Robert, *New Directions for Parents of Persons Who Are Retarded,* Abingdon Press.
Pierson, James, *77 Dynamic Ideas for the Christian Education of the Handicapped,* Standard Publishing.
Towns, Elmer L. and Groff, Roberta L., *Successful Ministry to the Retarded,* Moody Press.